FLIPPED ENGLISH DICTIONARY
NEW EDITION

An Easy Tool for Searching English Words of Desired Word Endings

A HANDY <u>REVERSE ORDER</u> WORD-SEARCH TOOL

Prof. Ratnakar Narale

Ratnaka℞

PUSTAK BHARATI

BOOKS-INDIA.COM

Author :
Dr. Ratnakar Narale
B.Sc. (Nagpur), M.Sc. (Pune), Ph.D. (IIT), Ph.D. (Kalidas Sanskrit Univ.);
Prof. Hindi, Ryerson University, Toronto.
web   : www.books-india.com
email : books.india.books@gmail.com

Title :
"Flipped English Dictionary, New Edition"
An Easy Tool for Searching English Words of Desired Word Endings.
This valuable resource word search tool, with over 30,000 selected words rearranged and grouped alphabetically **based on their spellings in reverse order starting from right to left**, provides an easy way for finding specific or rhyming words. This Dictionary is useful for Students, Teachers, Writers, Poets, Crossword Solvers, Special Education Professionals and Communication Disorder Specialists.

Published by :
BOOKS-INDIA (PUSTAK BHARATI)
  Division of PC PLUS Ltd.,

For :
Sanskrit Hindi Research Institute, Toronto

Copyright © 2014
ISBN 978-1-897416-62-4

ISBN 978-1-897416-62-4
90000

9 781897 416624

Dedicated to

My Loving Grandchildren
Samay, Sahas, Saanjh, Saaya, Naksh, Nyra, Navay Narale

INDEX

How to use this book

PREFACE

This valuable resource word search tool, with over 30,000 selected words rearranged and grouped alphabetically **based on their spellings in reverse order starting from right to left**, provides an easy way for finding specific or rhyming words. This Dictionary is useful for Students, Teachers, Writers, Poets, Crossword Solvers, Special Education Professionals and Communication Disorder Specialists.

30,000 common useful words of the English language are carefully chosen for inclusion in this Dictionary. These chosen words are 'flip-sorted' in their reverse spelling order, starting with the ending of the word progressing the sequence towards the beginning of the words.

These flip-sorted words are then grouped in the orders of words ending in A, B, C ...to Z. Then these grouped words are sub-grouped alphabetically in smaller groups for ease of search in smaller lists.

Finally, within each list of the sub-group, the words are shown in their usual dictionary order for the ease of their search, as shown : the first group (ba-ha) starts with word ending in ba, then ca, cca, ica, lica, mica, ...da, ea, ...to ha; then the next group (ia-na) has words starting with ia, ka, la, ...to na. followed by the group (oq-za) that starts wit words ending in oa to za. Similarly the next group (ab-ub) starts with the words ending in ab, eb, ib ...to ub and so on for words ending in b, then for the words ending in c, d, e, ... and finally az, dz, ez ...to zz.

Many writers and authors have used this tool for their literary works with great joy and sigh.

THE FLIPPED ENGLISH DICTIONARY
NEW EDITION

A DICTIONARY IN FLIP-REVERSE ORDER

1. WORDS ENDING IN LETTER - A

ba-ha

scuba yucca silica basilica replica mica arnica pica sciatica erotica exotica tapioca circa armada propaganda panda veranda memoranda addenda agenda anaconda rotunda pagoda barracuda idea trachea lea flea plea pea area urea sea overseas nausea tea sofa saga omega yoga alpha

ia-na

phobia fascia encyclopedia media cyclopedia nostalgia paraphernalia cilia mania egomania nymphomania insignia gloxinia insomnia ammonia paranoia utopia myopia aria malaria hypochondria diphtheria bacteria criteria hysteria euphoria emporia atria nutria aphasia amnesia fuchsia symposia ambrosia dyspepsia militia amentia dementia inertia via trivia alluvia anorexia pyrexia anoxia asphyxia paprika swastika bazooka impala voila umbrella vanilla guerilla flotilla villa medulla parabola gondola areola pergola gladiola viola cupola nebula fibula formula peninsula spatula tarantula fistula pajama llama mama drama melodrama panorama grandma edema anathema magma stigma dogma asthma gamma dilemma coma diploma aroma stoma karma plasma charisma mahatma trauma puma parenchyma banana iguana nirvana duodena phenomena subpoena arena hyena lamina

1

stamina retina ulna antenna corona fauna lacuna myna

oa-za

boa tiara algebra cerebra vertebra zebra cobra era cholera camera chimera genera tempera opera sera infra flora aurora stomata errata strata beta theta excreta capita delta placenta magenta junta iota quota septa aorta canasta vendetta aqua lava guava saliva nova larva bonanza stanza

2. WORDS ENDING IN LETTER - B

ab-ub

scab dab gab jab flab slab nab crab drab grab tab stab squab swab ebb bleb web bib fib jib glib nib rib crib drib midrib squib bulb jamb lamb limb climb bomb comb catacomb honeycomb rhomb aplomb entomb womb succumb dumb thumb plumb numb crumb bob cob fob gob hob job lob blob glob slob mob hobnob knob snob rob throb sob barb garb herb superb verb adverb reverb proverb orb absorb adsorb suburb curb blurb perturb disturb exurb cub hub club flub snub rub scrub drub grub shrub sub tub stub

3. WORDS ENDING IN LETTER - C

ac-nic zodiac cardiac maniac demoniac hypochondriac shellac tarmac almanac sac xebec spec sec exec mosaic monosyllabic rhombic phobic aerobic cubic thoracic nomadic sporadic dyadic medic comedic acidic fluidic skaldic methodic periodic melodic spasmodic prosodic traffic pacific specific prolific honorific terrific horrific scientific magic tragic paraplegic strategic neuralgic anagogic logic dialogic illogic geologic morphologic biologic lethargic synergic anarchic hierarchic psychic graphic philosophic hieroglyphic empathic ethic public republic cyclic relic exilic metallic idyllic parabolic symbolic hyperbolic melancholic frolic garlic hydraulic dynamic thermodynamic ceramic panoramic academic epidemic pandemic endemic polemic anemic systemic toxemic logarithmic rhythmic bulimic mimic comic gnomic economic autonomic atomic anatomic seismic cosmic microcosmic volcanic oceanic organic inorganic mechanic manic talismanic panic satanic botanic galvanic picnic scenic photogenic dysgenic eugenic hygienic unhygienic ethnic clinic bubonic phonic ionic bionic demonic hegemonic mnemonic harmonic canonic chronic ironic moronic electronic sonic subsonic tonic isotonic plutonic embryonic tunic cynic

oic-sic heroic azoic epic microscopic tropic topic isotopic aspic barbaric fabric hemispheric atmospheric cleric isomeric turmeric mesmeric numeric generic enteric neoteric esoteric hysteric euphoric rhetoric historic prehistoric electric metric symmetric geometric isometric volumetric citric eccentric concentric gastric uric mercuric panegyric lyric basic intrinsic extrinsic classic music physic

tic-etic tic adiabatic acrobatic pancreatic aliphatic emphatic lymphatic sciatic prelatic dramatic melodramatic thematic emblematic problematic systematic unsystematic phlegmatic enigmatic astigmatic dogmatic asthmatic climatic epigrammatic idiomatic axiomatic diplomatic aromatic chromatic monochromatic polychromatic somatic symptomatic automatic spermatic miasmatic prismatic rheumatic pneumatic fanatic morganatic lunatic hepatic idiosyncratic democratic aristocratic autocratic quadratic operatic erratic static ecstatic hydrostatic aquatic vatic didactic lactic galactic tactic hectic eclectic apoplectic an eutectic arctic alphabetic diabetic acetic ascetic eidetic geodetic exegetic apologetic energetic prophetic bathetic pathetic apathetic sympathetic unsympathetic antithetic parenthetic esthetic aesthetic athletic emetic arithmetic mimetic hermetic cosmetic genetic splenetic frenetic magnetic electromagnetic kinetic phonetic poetic onomatopoetic paretic heretic theoretic diaphoretic diuretic pyretic antipyretic peripatetic dietetic

itic-rtic rachitic mephitic enclitic politic impolitic eremitic hermitic critic diacritic nephritic arthritic parasitic basaltic cultic antic pedantic gigantic sycophantic transatlantic mantic semantic romantic necromantic unromantic frantic authentic chaotic robotic narcotic zygotic dichotic biotic idiotic meiotic semiotic amniotic patriotic osmotic cyanotic hypnotic despotic necrotic erotic sclerotic neurotic an mitotic amitotic exotic quixotic synaptic skeptic cataleptic epileptic peptic dyspeptic septic aseptic antiseptic ecliptic elliptic optic synoptic apocalyptic cryptic styptic cathartic aortic

stic-vtsc bombastic sarcastic ecclesiastic enthusiastic elastic scholastic plastic mastic gymnastic monastic dynastic spastic drastic periphrastic fantastic majestic domestic archaistic sadistic deistic theistic pantheistic monotheistic polytheistic logistic syllogistic eulogistic cabalistic idealistic realistic socialistic materialistic anomalistic journalistic fatalistic capitalistic individualistic evangelistic pugilistic nihilistic holistic simplistic somnambulistic pessimistic optimistic agonistic antagonistic monistic communistic egoistic Eucharistic characteristic aphoristic patristic belletristic juristic egotistic artistic inartistic autistic linguistic altruistic atavistic agnostic prognostic acrostic caustic encaustic acoustic rustic cystic mystic attic therapeutic epiphytic analytic paralytic catalytic hydrolytic histolytic

vic-isc civic pelvic ataxic dyslexic anorexic anoxic toxic nontoxic talc franc zinc sync doc manioc bloc roc havoc arc marc disc

4. WORDS ENDING IN LETTER - D

| ad-ead |

bad cad dad granddad doodad aoudad crawdad bead dead undead head ahead subhead deadhead redhead acidhead godhead hardhead behead bonehead forehead sorehead figurehead whitehead egghead blockhead bulkhead railhead wellhead bullhead drumhead maidenhead skinhead pinhead spearhead warhead dunderhead copperhead overhead airhead hogshead meathead flathead hothead masthead towhead lead plead mislead mead knead read bread beebread gingerbread sweetbread dread reread proofread thread rethread unthread unread spread widespread overspread outspread misread tread retread stead roadstead bedstead homestead farmstead instead

| fad-dd |

fad gad egad had shad naiad jeremiad triad myriad lad salad clad ironclad unclad glad ballad mad nomad maenad gonad monad goad load freeload reload caseload offload workload armload unload download shipload upload carload overload busload boatload cartload payload road broad abroad highroad railroad inroad crossroad byroad toad pad kneepad notepad footpad keypad farad brad grad tetrad sad tad pentad quad squad wad tightwad dyad dryad add odd

| ed-wed |

bed abed seabed deathbed embed waterbed riverbed flatbed hotbed geed heed bleed need kneed speed reed breed inbreed creed screed seed guaranteed steed weed tweed wed

| aid-oid |

aid laid inlaid mislaid maid paid raid braid afraid said bid rabid underbid overbid forbid morbid turbid outbid acid placid nonacid monoacid antacid flaccid rancid viscid lucid pellucid did redid candid splendid undid overdid sordid outdid katydid bifid rigid frigid algid turgid hid orchid aphid kid grandkid skid nonskid lid squalid valid invalid gelid annelid eyelid pallid solid semisolid nonsolid stolid slid backslid mid amid pyramid timid humid tumid arachnid hominid amoeboid rhomboid discoid lymphoid typhoid alkaloid tabloid cycloid myeloid colloid haploid diploid triploid celluloid sigmoid humanoid paranoid adenoid sphenoid solenoid hominoid lipoid anthropoid fibroid android hydroid spheroid aneroid steroid asteroid sangfroid ochroid thyroid ellipsoid sinusoid planetoid deltoid mastoid void avoid devoid nevoid ovoid hyoid schizoid rhizoid

pid-vid

rapid sapid vapid intrepid tepid lipid insipid limpid torpid hispid bicuspid cupid stupid rid arid semiarid hybrid acrid grid florid horrid torrid putrid lurid caryatid fetid carotid inter parotid plastid languid fluid quid liquid illiquid squid druid avid gravid livid vivid fervid

ald-uld

bald piebald ribald skewbald scald weald herald emerald geld held handheld beheld withheld upheld field midfield battlefield infield cornfield chesterfield airfield outfield hayfield shield wield yield meld weld gild wergild child grandchild godchild stepchild mild build rebuild guild wild old bold kobold overbold cold scold fold blindfold threefold refold gatefold fivefold scaffold manifold multifold billfold fanfold enfold tenfold unfold twofold sheepfold fourfold eightfold gold marigold hold handhold behold freehold toehold household stronghold withhold uphold threshold foothold cuckold mold remold sold resold unsold oversold outsold told retold foretold untold world would underworld auld could should mould would

and and band contraband headband waveband neckband armband disband husband hatband waistband wristband radicand brigand hand behindhand freehand forehand beforehand offhand longhand backhand deckhand dockhand farmhand unhand underhand overhand shorthand cowhand viand land bland badland headland midland woodland eland tideland homeland pineland foreland gland gangland highland backland parkland dreamland farmland inland mainland cropland upland garland nor fatherland hinterland overland moorland island flatland wetland meadowland lowland fairyland demand remand reprimand command summand gourmand expand brand firebrand misbrand operand grand errand strand sand thousand stand washstand withstand inkstand understand misunderstand wand

end end bend backbend unbend ascend descend condescend transcend addend dividend fend defend offend legend reprehend comprehend apprehend misapprehend fiend friend befriend weekend bookend lend blend mend amend emend commend recommend depend vilipend stipend impend append spend misspend outspend suspend upend expend rend yearend reverend trend send godsend tend subtend pretend intend superintend contend bartend portend distend attend extend coextend minuend vend wend

ind bind rebind unbind rescind find hind behind kind mankind womankind unkind blind purblind mind remind mastermind rind tamarind grind regrind wind headwind woodwind rewind tailwind whirlwind unwind downwind upwind

ond-und bond vagabond second abscond fond plafond blond diamond almond pond fishpond millpond despond respond correspond frond beyond moribund fecund rubicund jocund fund refund dachshund bound abound icebound hidebound rebound spellbound inbound unbound outbound redound found dumfound confound unfound profound newfound hound bloodhound horehound sleuthhound elkhound foxhound greyhound mound pound impound compound propound expound round around ground aground reground foreground background underground playground surround sound resound unsound astound wound rewound unwound gerund obtund rotund orotund

od
cod lingcod tomcod god demigod shod unshod slipshod method period clod plod mod nod synod food seafood nonfood good hood childhood falsehood statehood selfhood hardihood likelihood livelihood girlhood manhood womanhood maidenhood motherhood brotherhood spinsterhood neighborhood monkshood knighthood priesthood widowhood babyhood boyhood blood lifeblood oxblood flood mood snood rood brood stood understood misunderstood wood deadwood redwood hardwood cordwood pinewood firewood rosewood dogwood brushwood teakwood sandalwood wormwood ironwood cottonwood buttonwood sapwood pulpwood basswood driftwood softwood heartwood boxwood plywood pod hexapod seedpod copepod bipod tripod brachiopod cephalopod arthropod gastropod rod scrod ramrod nimrod prod trod hotrod sod fantod

ard-ird
bard tabard scabbard bombard card placard timecard bankcard discard postcard keycard standard beard graybeard heard reheard unheard overheard misheard regard disregard haggard laggard niggard sluggard hard chard pilchard clochard orchard diehard shard blowhard billiard milliard poniard tankard drunkard lard mallard collard pollard

dullard interlard foulard nard canard spikenard board aboard seaboard headboard cardboard sideboard baseboard pasteboard aboveboard pegboard switchboard splashboard blackboard signboard inboard onboard clapboard shipboard cupboard larboard starboard checkerboard overboard chessboard outboard keyboard hoard leopard mansard petard retard dotard leotard bastard dastard bustard custard mustard guard mudguard safeguard splashguard blackguard vanguard bodyguard jacquard boulevard

ard-ird ward award seaward windward sideward leeward homeward reward shoreward steward earthward northward southward backward awkward heavenward inward onward downward coward forward toward untoward upward rearward afterward forward henceforward thenceforward straightforward sward greensward leftward eastward northeastward westward southwestward outward wayward skyward yard vineyard graveyard churchyard backyard dockyard junkyard halyard steelyard schoolyard farmyard lanyard barnyard shipyard boatyard courtyard hazard haphazard lizard wizard gizzard blizzard buzzard halberd herd shepherd potsherd goatherd cowherd nerd bird seabird redbird firebird lyrebird bluebird lovebird kingbird songbird jailbird ovenbird catbird cowbird snowbird ladybird weird gird begird engird third

ord-urd cord accord disaccord record rerecord concord whipcord ripcord discord ford afford oxford chord harpsichord notochord fiord fjord lord landlord milord slumlord warlord overlord word headword reword foreword loanword sword password cussword byword keyword buzzword curd gourd surd absurd

ud-vd

baud laud applaud maraud fraud defraud bud rosebud cud scud dud feud thud mud loud aloud cloud becloud thundercloud overloud shroud enshroud proud spud crud stud bawd lewd shrewd crowd overcrowd alkyd

5. WORDS ENDING IN LETTER - E

ae-be
amoebae succubae thecae sundae tracheae cochleae foveae reggae algae tibiae fasciae scoriae minutiae lamellae patellae papillae maxillae medullae nebulae fibulae maculae formulae scapulae fistulae drachmae ulnae alumnae antennae personae faunae lacunae pupae brae vertebrae umbrae hetaerae amphorae florae pleurae caesurae tae setae vitae vulvae novae larvae babe glebe plebe phoebe grebe imbibe gibe jibe bribe

scribe ascribe subscribe describe prescribe circumscribe transcribe inscribe tribe diatribe vibe buncombe adobe lobe globe earlobe robe microbe wardrobe aerobe anaerobe bathrobe enrobe probe disrobe strobe cube jujube lube rube tube maybe

ace
ace dace peace face boldface deface paleface typeface reface preface efface surface outface lace palace shoelace necklace enlace unlace solace place replace fireplace birthplace commonplace displace misplace marketplace anyplace interlace bootlace populace mace grimace menace furnace pace apace carapace space subspace airspace outpace race brace embrace grace scapegrace disgrace tailrace millrace terrace trace retrace footrace

ece
fleece niece grandniece piece apiece headpiece codpiece timepiece eyepiece mouthpiece mantelpiece tailpiece altarpiece masterpiece frontispiece crosspiece

ice
ice plaice dice jaundice bodice cowardice prejudice benefice office suffice edifice sacrifice orifice artifice lice

chalice malice police accomplice surplice splice slice mice dormice titmice pumice nice overnice cornice choice rejoice voice invoice precipice coppice spice allspice hospice auspice rice avarice thrice licorice liquorice price caprice trice practice malpractice poultice entice prentice apprentice notice armistice solstice interstice justice injustice lattice juice sluice vice advice device crevice novice service disservice twice

| **ance** | disturbance significance insignificance dance riddance abidance avoidance guidance attendance abundance superabundance accordance discordance vengeance |

extravagance elegance arrogance chance perchance mischance enhance ambiance insouciance radiance defiance affiance allegiance valiance reliance alliance dalliance misalliance brilliance compliance appliance variance luxuriance deviance askance lance balance counterbalance overbalance nonchalance valance semblance resemblance glance vigilance surveillance parlance ambulance petulance romance performance nonperformance ordnance penance maintenance countenance discountenance appurtenance sustenance malignance repugnance ordinance finance predominance resonance consonance forbearance clearance appearance reappearance nonappearance disappearance remembrance encumbrance hindrance protuberance exuberance preponderance sufferance furtherance intolerance temperance intemperance utterance severance perseverance deliverance fragrance ignorance prance trance entrance remonstrance durance endurance insurance assurance reassurance defeasance malfeasance complaisance obeisance nuisance renaissance reconnaissance reactance inductance reluctance inhabitance exorbitance precipitance inheritance exultance repentance acquaintance acceptance importance unimportance stance substance distance resistance assistance circumstance instance admittance remittance pittance quittance nuance continuance discontinuance pursuance issuance advance grievance connivance contrivance observance nonobservance allowance abeyance conveyance purveyance joyance annoyance clairvoyance cognizance recognizance incognizance

ence complacence magnificence munificence reticence innocence nascence renascence pubescence iridescence incandescence quiescence acquiescence coalescence convalescence adolescence evanescence excrescence phosphorescence inflorescence fluorescence deliquescence effervescence reminiscence translucence cadence decadence precedence antecedence credence accidence coincidence diffidence confidence overconfidence subsidence residence evidence providence improvidence transcendence dependence independence superintendence correspondence impudence prudence imprudence jurisprudence fence offence indigence negligence diligence intelligence indulgence overindulgence effulgence emergence divergence convergence hence thence whence faience ambience science nescience prescience omniscience conscience obedience disobedience expedience audience salience resilience lenience convenience inconvenience sapience incipience percipience experience inexperience patience impatience sentience valence prevalence equivalence silence pestilence excellence indolence condolence violence somnolence insolence malevolence benevolence turbulence opulence corpulence virulence purulence flatulence vehemence commence recommence permanence eminence preeminence imminence prominence continence incontinence impertinence abstinence pence sixpence

renc deference reference preference difference indifference circumference inference conference interference transference adherence inherence coherence incoherence reverence irreverence abhorrence occurrence recurrence concurrence absence presence omnipresence essence quintessence competence incompetence pretence penitence renitence sentence omnipotence impotence inadvertence subsistence insistence consistence persistence existence nonexistence affluence effluence influence sequence subsequence consequence inconsequence eloquence grandiloquence magniloquence congruence mince prince since quince evince convince province wince

once
once sconce ensconce nonce dunce ounce bounce jounce flounce enounce denounce renounce announce pronounce pounce trounce scarce farce fierce pierce transpierce tierce amerce commerce coerce force enforce perforce divorce source resource acquiesce coalesce evanesce effervesce dehisce sauce duce traduce adduce educe deduce reduce seduce induce conduce produce reproduce introduce deuce puce prepuce spruce truce lettuce

ade-ede
bade forbade facade saccade decade barricade cavalcade brocade arcade cascade ambuscade limeade fade renegade brigade shade sunshade nightshade jade cockade blockade stockade lade marmalade blade glade enfilade fusillade unlade accolade overlade roulade made handmade homemade remade manmade unmade pomade esplanade promenade serenade grenade marinade colonnade gasconade lemonade cannonade escapade spade charade parade abrade masquerade grade degrade centigrade retrograde upgrade tirade comrade trade balustrade palisade glissade crusade rodomontade persuade dissuade evade invade pervade wade cede accede recede

precede secede antecede concede intercede millipede stampede impede supersede suede

ide-nde aide bide abide carbide decide regicide homicide germicide parricide patricide fratricide insecticide feticide infanticide suicide coincide ecocide biocide genocide iodide sulfide confide hide chide rawhide cowhide halide nuclide elide glide collide slide landslide mudslide backslide amide bromide cyanide actinide snide ride bride hydride anhydride deride chloride hydrochloride fluoride pride override nitride stride astride bestride outride telluride hayride joyride side aside seaside curbside subside roadside broadside bedside beside lakeside reside fireside preside offside ringside alongside backside dockside hillside poolside inside downside glycoside topside upside underside waterside riverside outside quayside wayside countryside tide betide eventide noontide peptide riptide guide misguide vide divide subdivide provide wide citywide oxide dioxide trioxide monoxide hydroxide peroxide allemande pitchblende hornblende blonde monde

ode ode bode abode forebode code decode encode miscode geode cathode diode triode lode implode explode mode commode incommode outmode node anode palinode dynode epode antipode rode erode overrode corrode electrode strode bestrode episode nematode horde

ude dude occlude preclude seclude include conclude exclude elude delude prelude allude collude interlude postlude nude denude seminude rude crude prude obtrude intrude protrude extrude transude etude quietude inquietude disquietude desuetude consuetude habitude solicitude longitude similitude verisimilitude solitude amplitude plenitude magnitude finitude definitude infinitude decrepitude turpitude lassitude vicissitude beatitude latitude platitude gratitude ingratitude exactitude inexactitude rectitude altitude multitude aptitude ineptitude promptitude certitude incertitude fortitude attitude servitude exude

ee bee freebee bumblebee honeybee emcee divorcee grandee standee attendee spondee fee coffee toffee gee squeegee negligee perigee pongee ogee apogee burgee refugee trochee debauchee garnishee banshee thee towhee lee melee flee glee jubilee expellee enrollee parolee coulee nee designee consignee assignee trainee detainee examinee nominee matinee knee internee returnee pee escapee epee teepee whoopee yippee toupee rupee dungaree decree referee conferee kedgeree free carefree agree disagree degree pedigree filigree three soiree retiree jamboree honoree spree tree shoetree rooftree entree puree see foresee advisee devisee licensee oversee endorsee fricassee lessee sightsee tee legatee manatee goatee evictee inductee draftee invitee guarantee grantee absentee patentee devotee repartee deportee enlistee trustee settee committee puttee suttee amputee tutee evacuee marquee levee jayvee wee peewee pewee payee employee chimpanzee

fe cafe chafe carafe strafe safe vouchsafe unsafe gaffe giraffe fife life midlife wildlife highlife lowlife knife penknife pocketknife rife strife wife midwife alewife housewife fishwife farmwife

age-page age cabbage cribbage garbage herbage cage birdcage boscage adage bandage appendage bondage poundage yardage cordage mileage lineage acreage leafage gage baggage luggage engage reengage greengage disengage mortgage roughage phage hemorrhage verbiage foliage carriage miscarriage marriage remarriage ferriage triage multiage leakage breakage soakage package wreckage dockage blockage linkage shrinkage assemblage pelage fuselage tutelage persiflage mucilage spoilage pupilage silage ensilage cartilage pillage spillage tillage village collage tollage haulage mage damage image pilgrimage rummage homage plumage orphanage manage teenage cozenage signage drainage vicinage badinage coinage tonnage peonage espionage commonage nonage baronage patronage parsonage personage carnage page seepage equipage rampage stumpage slippage stoppage

rage   rage vicarage garage disparage umbrage underage peerage steerage brokerage amperage average beverage leverage overage coverage sewerage suffrage saxifrage mirage enrage forage anchorage floorage moorage storage tutorage barrage demurrage outrage courage encourage discourage pasturage

sage   sage presage visage envisage dosage corsage massage passage message dressage usage sausage misusage

tage   hermitage heritage fruitage voltage vantage advantage disadvantage percentage clientage parentage mintage vintage montage frontage sabotage dotage footage potage cartage shortage portage stage wastage offstage onstage hostage postage upstage wattage cottage pottage outage language assuage cleavage ravage savage salvage selvage wage sewage flowage towage stowage swage drayage voyage

dge   badge cadge edge hedge ledge fledge pledge sledge knowledge acknowledge foreknowledge dredge sedge straightedge selvedge wedge midge ridge bridge abridge drawbridge fridge porridge cartridge partridge dodge lodge dislodge budge fudge judge adjudge prejudge misjudge kludge sludge smudge nudge drudge grudge begrudge trudge

ege-enge liege siege besiege sacrilege privilege allege college renege cortege beige oblige disoblige prestige vestige bilge bulge indulge divulge change interchange exchange phalange flange mange blancmange range midrange derange grange orange arrange rearrange disarrange strange estrange challenge avenge scavenge revenge lozenge binge hinge unhinge impinge cringe fringe infringe syringe singe tinge twinge sponge lunge plunge lounge scrounge expunge grunge

oge-ouge loge horologe scrooge stooge barge charge recharge undercharge surcharge discharge large enlarge concierge merge submerge emerge reemerge remerge immerge serge verge diverge converge dirge forge gorge engorge disgorge urge splurge scourge purge spurge surge upsurge gauge misgauge refuge febrifuge subterfuge huge deluge kluge gouge rouge

che-the ache cache headache toothache backache panache apache earache heartache mustache moustache gouache fiche cliche niche pastiche quiche avalanche brioche cloche troche menarche gauche penuche douche capuche ruche psyche strophe catastrophe apostrophe she the bathe sunbathe scathe sheathe breathe wreathe lathe loathe swathe seethe teethe lithe blithe writhe tithe nepenthe absinthe clothe unclothe soothe scythe

ie freebie zombie specie die caddie oldie organdie goodie birdie nudie hoagie budgie baggie veggie doggie bogie boogie stogie toughie mashie smoothie quickie talkie hankie pinkie junkie bookie cookie rookie lie goalie belie collie coolie stoolie underlie overlie girlie ramie preemie commie bonhomie anomie stymie beanie weenie genie wienie bonnie brownie townie pie magpie porkpie crappie preppie hippie yuppie sharpie potpie groupie brie aerie camaraderie eerie menagerie lingerie gaucherie diablerie causerie cha coterie grotesquerie reverie prairie calorie curie bourgeoisie lassie tootsie jalousie tie sweetie retie softie necktie sheltie untie auntie bootie cootie sortie cutie vie movie nixie pixie

ke   bake clambake cake teacake seedcake griddlecake beefcake pancake cupcake hotcake johnnycake fake hake shake handshake lake flake slake make remake unmake snake rattlesnake rake brake drake mandrake muckrake strake sake namesake keepsake forsake take betake retake intake uptake partake undertake overtake stake mistake sweepstake outtake quake seaquake earthquake wake awake reawake eke bike dike hike like alike unalike tomblike herblike saclike childlike godlike birdlike treelike lifelike knifelike snakelike needlelike homelike apelike ropelike viselike flutelike wavelike eyelike mazelike gauzelike songlike suchlike fishlike deathlike rocklike dreamlike gemlike fanlike manlike workmanlike statesmanlike sportsmanlike swanlike finlike moonlike fernlike unlike liplike hooplike warlike flowerlike dislike glasslike businesslike catlike netlike nutlike ladylike fairylike mike pike turnpike shunpike spike shrike strike tike yarmulke coke choke artichoke joke bloke smoke poke spoke bespoke misspoke cowpoke slowpoke broke stroke sunstroke upstroke toke stoke evoke revoke invoke convoke provoke woke awoke yoke unyoke burke rebuke duke archduke juke fluke nuke puke netsuke dyke tyke

ale   ale bale timbale musicale locale percale scale upscale dale gale regale farthingale nightingale hale inhale shale whale narwhale exhale kale male tamale female finale rationale pale impale chorale morale sale wholesale resale presale tale folktale telltale stale vale wale pinwale gunwale

| **able** | able bribable indescribable probable improbable absorbable imperturbable cable implacable ineradicable |

applicable inapplicable inexplicable amicable communicable despicable practicable impracticable irrevocable educable readable tradable biddable formidable unavoidable foldable moldable bendable commendable dependable fordable laudable

| **eable** | peaceable ineffaceable replaceable traceable noticeable unnoticeable serviceable unserviceable pronounceable |

agreeable disagreeable seeable manageable unmanageable changeable unchangeable interchangeable chargeable likeable saleable malleable nameable permeable impermeable fineable useable dateable loveable moveable

sizeable fable affable ineffable gable indefatigable navigable impeachable unimpeachable teachable irreproachable unapproachable detachable unquenchable laughable cashable washable fishable punishable perishable imperishable distinguishable

| **iable** | appreciable inappreciable sociable unsociable remediable irremediable classifiable unclassifiable |

justifiable unjustifiable liable reliable pliable amiable deniable undeniable variable invariable friable satiable insatiable pitiable negotiable dutiable viable enviable

| **kabl** | unspeakable breakable shakable mistakable |

unmistakable lockable likable bankable thinkable unthinkable sinkable remarkable workable scalable healable salable sailable unassailable available unavailable reconcilable irreconcilable callable fellable sellable billable tillable controllable uncontrollable syllable monosyllable violable inviolable inconsolable incalculable blamable namable unnamable tamable untamable redeemable irredeemable reclaimable irreclaimable estimable inestimable inflammable dimmable unfathomable farmable formable conformable presumable enable inalienable amenable tenable untenable pregnable impregnable explainable trainable obtainable ascertainable attainable unattainable finable definable indefinable imaginable unimaginable abominable terminable interminable damnable winnable pardonable unpardonable unconscionable fashionable unfashionable companionable impressionable actionable objectionable unobjectionable unmentionable exceptionable unexceptionable questionable unquestionable reasonable unreasonable treasonable seasonable unseasonable personable atonable governable ungovernable burnable unable tunable doable undoable capable incapable palpable impalpable culpable inculpable ungraspable

| **rable** | arable bearable unbearable hearable wearable sharable declarable parable reparable irreparable separable inseparable comparable incomparable execrable |

considerable inconsiderable imponderable referable preferable sufferable insufferable transferable decipherable tolerable intolerable numerable innumerable venerable vulnerable invulnerable operable insuperable miserable unalterable unutterable unconquerable irrecoverable discoverable undiscoverable answerable unanswerable hirable admirable desirable undesirable adorable colorable deplorable memorable honorable dishonorable storable restorable favorable unfavorable inexorable penetrable impenetrable demonstrable curable incurable procurable durable endurable unendurable pleasurable measurable immeasurable commensurable incommensurable insurable sable unappeasable increasable erasable exercisable disable merchandisable advisable inadvisable devisable revisable condensable indispensable transposable passable impassable usable excusable inexcusable reusable unusable

rable table abatable debatable datable eatable untreatable palatable unpalatable translatable ratable redoubtable tractable retractable intractable delectable respectable indictable ineluctable getable vegetable timetable retable bitable habitable inhabitable uninhabitable dubitable indubitable excitable editable creditable discreditable profitable unprofitable illimitable inimitable indomitable hospitable charitable uncharitable heritable inheritable veritable irritable equitable inequitable suitable unsuitable inevitable worktable merchantable tenantable unwarrantable lamentable presentable accountable unaccountable discountable surmountable insurmountable notable bootable potable quotable adaptable acceptable unacceptable comfortable uncomfortable portable supportable insupportable unsupportable stable testable detestable contestable incontestable constable unstable adjustable gettable regrettable attributable executable refutable irrefutable mutable immutable reputable disreputable computable disputable indisputable inscrutable arguable valuable invaluable equable pursuable

vable savable unachievable believable unbelievable irretrievable receivable conceivable inconceivable livable derivable salvable solvable unsolvable lovable movable removable immovable provable observable chewable viewable allowable knowable unknowable taxable fixable mixable

24

playable payable unswayable flyable enjoyable realizable recognizable sizable babble dabble gabble rabble scrabble grabble squabble pebble dibble nibble scribble dribble quibble bobble cobble gobble hobble wobble bubble rubble stubble feeble enfeeble treble

ible bible invincible convincible coercible forcible irascible miscible educible deducible reducible irreducible crucible edible inedible credible incredible mandible extendible vendible audible inaudible legible illegible eligible negligible intelligible unintelligible dirigible incorrigible tangible intangible fungible indelible fallible infallible gullible discernible indiscernible foible terrible horrible feasible infeasible inevasible risible visible divisible indivisible invisible indefensible reprehensible comprehensible apprehensible sensible insensible ostensible extensible responsible irresponsible reversible irreversible impassible accessible inaccessible repressible irrepressible impressible compressible inexpressible admissible inadmissible remissible permissible transmissible possible impossible plausible fusible infusible compatible incompatible contractible indefectible collectible deductible destructible indestructible perceptible imperceptible susceptible unsusceptible contemptible corruptible incorruptible convertible digestible indigestible irresistible inexhaustible combustible incombustible flexible inflexible

ible amble preamble gamble shamble ramble bramble scramble tremble resemble ensemble assemble dissemble thimble nimble bumble fumble humble jumble mumble rumble crumble grumble tumble stumble noble ignoble ennoble garble marble warble burble bauble soluble insoluble indissoluble voluble double redouble trouble ruble chasuble

cle debacle treacle manacle binnacle pinnacle barnacle tabernacle miracle spiracle oracle coracle spectacle pentacle tentacle receptacle obstacle cubicle icicle fascicle pedicle vehicle pellicle follicle panicle chronicle ventricle utricle auricle vesicle canticle article particle testicle cuticle clavicle uncle carbuncle peduncle granduncle furuncle monocle tubercle circle semicircle encircle muscle corpuscle boucle cycle recycle bicycle unicycle epicycle tricycle

dle beadle treadle ladle cradle addle paddle straddle saddle sidesaddle unsaddle waddle swaddle twaddle meddle intermeddle peddle diddle fiddle middle piddle riddle griddle twiddle coddle toddle cuddle fuddle befuddle huddle muddle puddle wheedle needle idle bridle unbridle sidle candle dandle handle manhandle bindle kindle rekindle enkindle spindle dwindle swindle fondle bundle rundle trundle boodle caboodle doodle noodle poodle girdle curdle hurdle dawdle dele allele ukulele clientele stele baffle snaffle raffle waffle sniffle piffle riffle scuffle shuffle muffle snuffle ruffle truffle rifle trifle stifle

gle eagle beagle finagle gaggle haggle draggle straggle waggle giggle jiggle sniggle wriggle squiggle wiggle boggle goggle joggle toggle juggle smuggle snuggle struggle inveigle angle bangle dangle triangle jangle mangle spangle bespangle quadrangle strangle wrangle tangle rectangle entangle disentangle untangle wangle dingle shingle jingle mingle intermingle single tingle bungle jungle ogle gargle burgle gurgle bugle pinochle

ile bile labile stabile mobile immobile automobile nubile facile imbecile domicile reconcile docile indocile crocodile audile file defile profile misfile agile fragile bibliophile while awhile worthwhile meanwhile erstwhile mile simile facsimile chamomile smile anile penile senile juvenile toile voile pile woodpile compile rile febrile sterile puerile virile scurrile laetrile ensile prehensile pensile tensile extensile sessile scissile fissile missile tile volatile versatile retractile contractile tactile projectile ductile retile mercantile infantile gentile quintile motile reptile quartile fertile infertile stile turnstile hostile utile futile inutile textile guile beguile vile revile servile wile exile flexile

| kle | cackle hackle shackle ramshackle crackle grackle tackle retackle deckle heckle speckle freckle fickle pickle prickle |

trickle sickle tickle stickle cockle buckle unbuckle chuckle knuckle truckle suckle honeysuckle ankle rankle crinkle sprinkle wrinkle tinkle periwinkle twinkle sparkle belle nacelle micelle villanelle quenelle demoiselle mademoiselle bagatelle nouvelle gazelle faille canaille reveille chenille quadrille grille pastille coquille vaudeville tulle

| ole | bole amphibole hyperbole dole condole aureole hole kneehole eyehole bunghole sinkhole hellhole armhole wormhole manhole pinhole pigeonhole buttonhole |

peephole loophole asshole knothole pothole porthole posthole whole blowhole foxhole keyhole oriole petiole cajole mole pole tadpole ridgepole flagpole dipole beanpole maypole role barcarole escarole rigmarole parole sole resole camisole insole console rissole stole diastole systole vacuole vole

| ple | maple staple steeple participle principle disciple maniple triple multiple ample trample sample resample ensample example temple dimple pimple simple wimple rumple |

crumple people townspeople co apple dapple pineapple scrapple grapple nipple ripple cripple tipple stipple topple stopple supple purple duple couple uncouple scruple quintuple sextuple merle isle aisle lisle hassle tussle tousle

<table>
<tr><td>

tle-zle

</td><td>

subtle unsubtle beetle title subtitle entitle cantle mantle gentle ungentle startle chortle hurtle turtle myrtle castle

</td></tr>
</table>

forecastle nestle pestle trestle wrestle thistle whistle epistle bristle gristle jostle apostle bustle hustle rustle battle embattle cattle rattle prattle tattle wattle fettle kettle mettle nettle settle resettle unsettle whittle skittle little belittle spittle brittle bottle rebottle bluebottle mottle throttle scuttle shuttle vestibule lobule globule tubule molecule ridicule reticule monticule animalcule schedule module nodule virgule cellule mule granule joule ampoule papule stipule rule ferule spherule ferrule overrule misrule capsule pustule ovule axle argyle gargoyle style restyle dazzle bedazzle frazzle embezzle fizzle drizzle frizzle sizzle swizzle nozzle guzzle muzzle nuzzle puzzle

<table>
<tr><td>

me

</td><td>

came became overcame dame beldame fame defame game endgame ballgame shame lame blame flame aflame

</td></tr>
</table>

enflame inflame name rename forename prename nickname penname surname misname byname frame reframe airframe same sesame selfsame tame acme raceme academe scheme grapheme morpheme blaspheme theme phoneme trireme supreme extreme dime regime chime lime sublime resublime clime birdlime quicklime slime mime pantomime anime rime crime grime begrime prime time bedtime seedtime lifetime sometime onetime retime aforetime halftime ragtime springtime longtime lunchtime maritime mealtime meantime centime noontime downtime uptime wartime summertime dinnertime overtime airtime pastime nighttime flextime daytime playtime anytime oriflamme femme come become welcome unwelcome income overcome outcome dome macrodome home biome genome gnome pome syndrome airdrome chrome monochrome polychrome some frolicsome handsome unhandsome blithesome troublesome meddlesome wholesome unwholesome mettlesome lonesome tiresome venturesome gruesome lovesome awesome loathsome toothsome noisome wearisome irksome quarrelsome toilsome fulsome burdensome winsome ribosome twosome fearsome bothersome foursome lissome lightsome tome epitome rhizome gendarme he pr fume perfume legume inhume exhume flume illume volume plume spume brume subsume resume presume consume assume reassume costume rhyme thyme enzyme coenzyme

ane bane henbane urbane cane chicane hurricane arcane mundane profane thane ethane methane urethane lane plane seaplane deplane biplane enplane hydroplane warplane airplane mane germane humane inhumane inane pane propane counterpane membrane crane sane tisane insane octane pentane butane vane wane hexane acne epicene scene obscene gene indigene phosgene hygiene scalene naphthalene ethylene acetylene serene gangrene neoprene isoprene terrene styrene kerosene carotene toluene trinitrotoluene convene reconvene supervene intervene pyroxene benzene nitrobenzene champagne cologne

ine cocaine procaine chatelaine romaine ptomaine migraine moraine woodbine combine recombine carbine turbine concubine cine vaccine internecine medicine porcine piscine oscine dine guanidine pyridine undine iodine sardine codeine caffeine seine fine define redefine refine confine superfine imagine engine chine machine trephine morphine dauphine shine moonshine sunshine outshine labyrinthine whine

line	line alkaline tourmaline praline saline hyaline cline decline recline incline disincline syncline deadline headline redline midline landline sideline beeline feline lifeline timeline

pipeline reline baseline dateline roofline aniline aquiline neckline crystalline sibylline streamline tramline hemline mainline crinoline gasoline discipline hipline marline underline interline airline hairline clothesline ratline buntline hotline outline masculine bowline towline byline skyline

min	mine amine famine gamine calamine melamine dopamine examine bromine carmine ermine undermine determine predetermine jasmine illumine nine canine guanine

adenine strychnine feminine unfeminine asinine quinine leonine saturnine heroine

pine	pine rapine repine alpine transalpine vulpine opine atropine spine porcupine lupine supine

rine	margarine saccharine marine ultramarine submarine nectarine brine exocrine alexandrine nitroglycerine ferine tangerine pelerine passerine uterine peregrine shrine

enshrine chorine chlorine fluorine trine latrine doctrine citrine urine figurine tambourine

sine	sine arcsine cuisine cosine tyrosine cytosine arsine ursine glassine limousine lysine tine palatine astatine saltine infantine galantine eglantine adamantine quarantine

dentine argentine serpentine turpentine tontine nicotine guillotine libertine destine predestine clandestine intestine philistine pristine routine sanguine linguine genuine equine vine ravine divine olivine ovine bovine corvine wine swine twine entwine untwine intertwine bombazine magazine julienne cayenne cretonne

one one bone whalebone herringbone fishbone wishbone backbone tailbone trombone shinbone hipbone jawbone cone pinecone silicone scone done redone condone undone underdone overdone outdone someone gone woebegone foregone undergone forgone bygone hone phone telephone gramophone microphone earphone shone outshone pr lone alone abalone clone cyclone anticyclone anemone hormone none rotenone pone cornpone propone postpone crone drone cicerone throne dethrone enthrone prone tone atone acetone halftone semitone baritone intone monotone peptone undertone overtone stone tombstone curbstone loadstone sandstone grindstone lodestone freestone milestone limestone gravestone touchstone hearthstone oilstone millstone gemstone brimstone moonstone ironstone capstone whetstone keystone anyone everyone zone rezone ozone caserne interne sauterne borne airborne forborne nocturne demesne

une tribune dune triune jejune immune commune rune prune tune retune fortune misfortune importune opportune inopportune mistune attune picayune dyne anodyne aerodyne oboe doe foe hoe backhoe shoe horseshoe gumshoe overshoe snowshoe pekoe aloe floe sloe canoe hoopoe roe throe toe mistletoe tiptoe woe

ape ape cape seascape landscape escape gape agape shape reshape shipshape misshape jape nape rape crape scrape drape undrape serape grape tape crepe recipe snipe pipe windpipe stovepipe bagpipe tailpipe panpipe hornpipe blowpipe ripe gripe unripe overripe tripe stripe wipe swipe cope syncope scope telescope stroboscope kaleidoscope stethoscope microscope horoscope fluoroscope spectroscope gyroscope dope hope calliope lope elope antelope envelope interlope slope aslope mope nope pope rope phalarope grope misanthrope trope towrope tope isotope frappe steppe grippe taupe dupe coupe loupe troupe drupe hype type subtype retype tintype ecotype stereotype logotype genotype monotype ferrotype electrotype mistype

are | are bare threadbare care scare dare fare thoroughfare welfare fanfare carfare warfare airfare hare chare share blare declare flare glare mare nightmare snare ensnare pare prepare compare spare rare curare tare hectare stare outstare square ware aware unaware hardware beware stoneware dishware cookware stemware firmware earthenware ovenware ironware slipware glassware flatware giftware software clayware

bre | macabre timbre hombre acre wiseacre nacre massacre chancre mediocre lucre cadre padre ere sincere insincere interfere here adhere inhere cohere sphere hemisphere lithosphere atmosphere hydrosphere there where somewhere elsewhere nowhere anywhere everywhere premiere derriere portiere mere cashmere ampere confrere sere austere revere severe persevere were gruyere ogre ochre euchre ire affaire millionaire concessionaire co solitaire dire fire afire wildfire surefire backfire hellfire bonfire gunfire campfire misfire spitfire foxfire hire rehire sapphire shire

ire | lire mire admire bemire quagmire pismire venire armoire conservatoire escritoire vampire empire umpire spire aspire respire inspire conspire perspire suspire expire sire grandsire desire tire satire retire entire overtire attire quire acquire require inquire squire esquire wire barbwire hardwire rewire tripwire

| **ore** | ore bore hellebore smoothbore overbore forbore core albacore hardcore encore score underscore fourscore outscore adore stevedore fore pinafore before therefore |

wherefore heretofore theretofore gore chore shore ashore seashore offshore inshore onshore whore lore galore folklore booklore deplore implore explore more sycamore sophomore furthermore evermore nevermore anymore ignore signore snore pore spore zoospore sore bedsore eyesore footsore tore store restore omnivore carnivore wore swore forswore outwore yore bizarre parterre theatre

| **ure** | cure sinecure secure insecure pedicure manicure epicure procure obscure procedure endure verdure ordure coiffure figure refigure prefigure disfigure brochure abjure adjure |

injure conjure perjure lure failure allure demure immure manure tenure inure pure impure sure pleasure displeasure measure treasure embrasure erasure leisure cocksure ensure censure insure reinsure tonsure unsure closure enclosure disclosure cynosure composure discomposure exposure assure reassure pressure fissure judicature caricature feature creature ligature miniature entablature nomenclature filature legislature mature premature immature armature nature denature signature temperature literature stature curvature manufacture fracture prefecture conjecture lecture architecture picture stricture cincture tincture juncture puncture structure understructure superstructure portraiture expenditure forfeiture discomfiture geniture furniture investiture culture apiculture agriculture floriculture horticulture sepulture vulture debenture denture indenture calenture venture adventure peradventure misadventure jointure cloture capture recapture rapture enrapture scripture sculpture rupture departure aperture overture torture nurture pasture gesture vesture moisture posture imposture future couture suture texture fixture mixture admixture commixture intermixture nervure flexure azure seizure oeuvre byre gyre lyre pyre

| **ase** | base abase database debase case seedcase bookcase encase incase uncase slipcase staircase suitcase nutcase showcase |

pillowcase ease cease decease surcease lease sublease nuclease release please displease unease appease crease decrease increase grease degrease disease tease protease chase steeplechase enchase purchase repurchase phase anaphase prophase ukase orthoclase amylase lipase erase esterase phrase paraphrase rephrase lactase maltase diastase vase obese diocese geese cheese these legalese manganese

| **ise** | malaise polonaise raise braise fraise praise appraise upraise precise circumcise incise concise exercise exorcise abscise excise paradise merchandise franchise enfranchise |

valise demise chemise remise premise promise compromise surmise anise noise poise equipoise counterpoise porpoise tortoise turquoise despise rise arise cerise moonrise sunrise reprise comprise apprise enterprise surprise treatise advertise mortise chastise guise disguise marquise bruise cruise vise advise devise televise revise improvise supervise wise crabwise endwise sidewise edgewise likewise lengthwise contrariwise unwise nowise stepwise otherwise crosswise anywise false else pulse repulse impulse expulse avulse convulse cleanse manse expanse license incense frankincense dense condense defense offense immense recompense dispense suspense expense sense nonsense tense pretense intense rinse response ribose verbose varicose jocose viscose glucose

| **ose-tse** | dose overdose hose chose metamorphose those whose |

grandiose foliose otiose lose close foreclose enclose unclose disclose cellulose ramose plumose lachrymose nose bluenose diagnose caboose goose mongoose choose loose unloose moose vamoose schmoose noose burnoose papoose pose depose repose adipose impose compose decompose discompose propose oppose suppose presuppose interpose purpose dispose indispose transpose expose rose arose sucrose tuberose primrose morose prose dextrose comatose lactose fructose maltose apse lapse elapse relapse collapse synapse traipse eclipse ellipse glimpse copse corpse hearse rehearse coarse hoarse parse sparse submerse immerse asperse disperse intersperse terse verse averse traverse obverse adverse reverse diverse universe inverse converse perverse transverse endorse indorse gorse horse unhorse sawhorse remorse worse reimburse disburse curse nurse bourse course recourse concourse watercourse intercourse discourse purse cutpurse masse impasse crevasse largesse noblesse finesse pelisse plisse fosse posse lacrosse mousse tsetse

| use |

use cause because clause applause pause abuse disabuse accuse excuse reuse chartreuse danseuse masseuse fuse defuse refuse effuse diffuse suffuse infuse confuse profuse perfuse enthuse recluse muse amuse bemuse hypotenuse nonuse douse house teahouse clubhouse chouse madhouse guardhouse icehouse coffeehouse alehouse warehouse storehouse statehouse doghouse washhouse blockhouse workhouse wheelhouse schoolhouse customhouse farmhouse greenhouse townhouse chophouse beerhouse summerhouse slaughterhouse poorhouse almshouse boathouse lighthouse penthouse hothouse courthouse nuthouse outhouse playhouse louse blouse delouse mouse dormouse titmouse spouse espouse rouse arouse carouse grouse souse ruse cruse peruse overuse abstruse disuse misuse obtuse contuse hawse dowse browse drowse

ate
ate bate abate debate rebate celibate globate probate reprobate acerbate incubate placate vacate desiccate defecate deprecate imprecate syllabicate eradicate abdicate dedicate medicate predicate indicate vindicate syndicate certificate delicate indelicate overdelicate silicate plicate replicate triplicate implicate complicate supplicate duplicate reduplicate communicate excommunicate prevaricate fabricate lubricate intricate extricate masticate domesticate sophisticate prognosticate intoxicate falcate defalcate inculcate truncate suffocate locate relocate allocate dislocate reciprocate advocate equivocate demarcate altercate bifurcate educate date gradate predate sedate antedate elucidate candidate validate invalidate consolidate dilapidate cuspidate liquidate backdate mandate emendate fecundate inundate accommodate update chordate misdate postdate outdate caudate ideate nucleate aculeate permeate delineate create recreate increate procreate aureate laureate baccalaureate roseate nauseate

fate
fate sulfate gate agate runagate propagate divagate variegate legate delegate relegate negate abnegate aggregate congregate obligate profligate fumigate frigate irrigate litigate mitigate castigate investigate instigate navigate tailgate tollgate promulgate vulgate elongate abrogate derogate arrogate interrogate surrogate objurgate billingsgate conjugate

hate
hate phosphate glaciate emaciate depreciate appreciate officiate enunciate annunciate associate dissociate excruciate radiate irradiate mediate immediate intermediate repudiate collegiate retaliate ciliate conciliate humiliate palliate foliate trifoliate calumniate opiate expiate inebriate seriate appropriate inappropriate striate infuriate luxuriate expatiate

ingratiate satiate initiate propitiate vitiate novitiate substantiate negotiate aviate obviate deviate alleviate exuviate skate

late late intercalate escalate palate oxalate ablate oblate elate relate prelate correlate deflate inflate conflate sibilate jubilate dilate annihilate assimilate ventilate mutilate flagellate vacillate oscillate scintillate collate chocolate percolate etiolate violate inviolate immolate interpolate desolate isolate insolate disconsolate plate endplate template contemplate tinplate breastplate slate translate tabulate ambulate somnambulate perambulate ejaculate maculate immaculate flocculate peculate speculate matriculate reticulate articulate inarticulate gesticulate calculate miscalculate inoculate circulate osculate adulate undulate modulate coagulate regulate ungulate pullulate ululate emulate simulate dissimulate stimulate formulate cumulate accumulate granulate stipulate copulate populate depopulate insulate congratulate capitulate recapitulate expostulate ovulate

mate mate bedmate cremate decimate sublimate climate acclimate animate reanimate inanimate primate legitimate illegitimate ultimate intimate estimate underestimate overestimate proximate approximate checkmate bunkmate palmate cellmate teammate roommate summate consummate inmate chromate automate shipmate helpmate messmate seatmate crewmate playmate permanganate planate emanate pomegranate alienate crenate senate arsenate rejuvenate agnate magnate stagnate impregnate designate cognate vaccinate fascinate hallucinate iodinate ordinate subordinate inordinate paginate originate alginate laminate contaminate staminate effeminate geminate disseminate eliminate incriminate discriminate indiscriminate culminate fulminate abominate dominate predominate nominate denominate germinate terminate determinate indeterminate illuminate ruminate marinate indoctrinate urinate assassinate procrastinate obstinate predestinate innate pinnate connate carbonate donate neonate phonate opinionate passionate compassionate dispassionate affectionate proportionate resonate personate detonate incarnate ternate alternate ornate fortunate unfortunate importunate inchoate benzoate pate baldpate anticipate participate emancipate dissipate palpate episcopate extirpate spate pupate

| **rate** | rate karate exhilarate separate disparate celebrate cerebrate vertebrate invertebrate vibrate lucubrate crate desecrate consecrate execrate uncrate quadrate hydrate aerate berate |

liberate deliberate cerate lacerate macerate ulcerate eviscerate federate confederate considerate inconsiderate moderate immoderate vociferate exaggerate refrigerate accelerate tolerate conglomerate numerate enumerate generate degenerate regenerate unregenerate venerate incinerate itinerate exonerate remunerate temperate intemperate operate cooperate exasperate desperate recuperate vituperate inveterate iterate literate obliterate illiterate transliterate adulterate asseverate overate grate migrate emigrate denigrate ingrate irate emirate pirate aspirate orate borate elaborate corroborate decorate perforate invigorate deteriorate chlorate commemorate evaporate corporate incorporate perorate prorate expectorate doctorate prate narrate underrate serrate overrate penetrate perpetrate citrate nitrate filtrate concentrate castrate fenestrate magistrate demonstrate remonstrate prostrate illustrate frustrate curate accurate inaccurate obdurate indurate inaugurate depurate suppurate commensurate maturate saturate supersaturate triturate gyrate butyrate

| **sate** | sate pulsate compensate sensate insensate lactate tractate |

dictate eructate hebetate acetate vegetate incapacitate resuscitate meditate premeditate agitate cogitate excogitate rehabilitate debilitate facilitate militate imitate decapitate crepitate precipitate palpitate irritate hesitate necessitate nictitate gravitate levitate dentate edentate commentate annotate rotate state devastate estate gestate restate testate instate apostate prostate upstate overstate misstate mutate amputate evacuate graduate undergraduate evaluate attenuate extenuate sinuate insinuate equate adequate inadequate infatuate actuate effectuate punctuate fluctuate perpetuate habituate situate accentuate excavate aggravate elevate recidivate salivate private activate cultivate motivate captivate solvate ovate renovate innovate enervate fixate

ete
fete effete exegete machete esthete aesthete delete athlete obsolete deplete replete complete incomplete mete gamete compete accrete secrete concrete discrete excrete

ite
bite fleabite backbite trilobite cenobite overbite frostbite cite anthracite recite calcite incite plebiscite excite overexcite expedite recondite hermaphrodite cordite erudite jadeite sulfite malachite graphite white bobwhite nonwhite kite blatherskite halite tantalite hyalite elite satellite polite impolite mite dynamite eremite stalagmite sodomite dolomite termite smite urbanite vulcanite granite stibnite ignite lignite finite definite indefinite infinite ebonite aconite taconite aragonite limonite ammonite unite reunite disunite spite despite respite rite barite sybarite hypocrite dendrite anhydrite marguerite nephrite laborite meteorite anchorite diorite chlorite fluorite favorite sprite ferrite trite nitrite contrite azurite write rewrite miswrite pyrite site parasite requisite perquisite exquisite composite apposite opposite campsite steatite hematite pegmatite ratite stalactite petite appetite tektite

argentite partite bipartite tripartite quite requite mesquite suite invite bauxite monazite svelte ante confidante andante dilettante debutante entente enceinte

ote cote dovecote dote anecdote antidote zygote matelote mote emote demote remote promote smote note endnote denote banknote connote footnote keynote capote compote rote garrote wrote rewrote miswrote creosote tote asymptote quote unquote misquote vote devote revote outvote peyote coyote carte forte pianoforte torte baste lambaste caste outcaste haste chaste unchaste paste taste foretaste distaste waste imp batiste artiste riposte latte matte serviette diskette palette novelette toilette roulette roomette kitchenette vignette lorgnette dinette marionette mignonette lunette brunette pipette cigarette aigrette barrette burette curette anisette rosette cassette quartette baguette silhouette pirouette etiquette banquette coquette statuette corvette layette gazette cocotte calotte gavotte butte

ute haute tribute contribute distribute attribute cute acute prosecute persecute execute refute confute chute parachute jute lute salute elute flute dilute pollute solute absolute resolute irresolute dissolute volute revolute convolute mute malamute commute permute minute comminute

oute route reroute misroute depute repute disrepute impute compute miscompute dispute brute hirsute statute substitute destitute institute constitute prostitute astute byte megabyte gigabyte kilobyte troglodyte epiphyte neophyte zoophyte proselyte acolyte electrolyte

ue imbue cue barbecue curlicue rescue miscue due subdue

residue endue fondue undue overdue queue ague league colleague plague vague segue gigue intrigue fatigue gangue harangue dengue meringue tongue pedagogue demagogue synagogue dialogue analogue catalogue eclogue epilogue collogue homologue monologue prologue rogue brogue drogue pirogue prorogue vogue argue reargue morgue fugue hue value devalue revalue undervalue overvalue blue clue flue glue unglue slue venue avenue revenue retinue continue discontinue moue macaque claque plaque al opaque fl oblique clique technique unique biunique pique physique critique antique mystique boutique bezique catafalque baroque toque torque masque arabesque burlesque picturesque grotesque statuesque bisque mosque brusque rue imbrue accrue true untrue construe sue ensue pursue issue reissue tissue statue virtue revue

ave-eve cave concave biconcave eave heave sheave leave cleave bereave weave reweave unweave interweave gave forgave have behave misbehave shave lave enclave conclave slave enslave nave knave soave pave repave rave brave crave grave engrave deprave architrave save octave stave suave wave airwave eve sleeve peeve reeve achieve thieve believe disbelieve misbelieve relieve grieve aggrieve reprieve retrieve sieve

ive naive waive coercive conducive dive khedive nosedive endive gerundive skydive deceive undeceive receive conceive misconceive perceive five give forgive hive chive archive beehive jive skive live alive relive olive outlive connive rive drive overdrive derive shrive thrive deprive arrive contrive strive

sive abrasive persuasive evasive invasive pervasive adhesive cohesive decisive incisive derisive divisive repulsive impulsive compulsive convulsive expansive defensive offensive inoffensive comprehensive apprehensive pensive expensive inexpensive intensive extensive responsive plosive implosive explosive erosive corrosive aversive subversive cursive discursive excursive massive passive impassive successive recessive excessive aggressive progressive retrogressive repressive impressive unimpressive compressive oppressive expressive inexpressive possessive missive submissive admissive emissive permissive abusive effusive diffusive inclusive conclusive inconclusive exclusive elusive delusive allusive illusive collusive obtrusive unobtrusive intrusive

tive combative indicative communicative locative vocative evocative provocative dative sedative creative procreative negative prerogative interrogative purgative depreciative appreciative palliative initiative talkative ablative relative correlative dilative contemplative superlative legislative speculative regulative cumulative accumulative recapitulative amative affirmative formative native sanative imaginative unimaginative discriminative nominative carminative opinionative alternative anticipative nuncupative reparative preparative comparative lucrative deliberative generative regenerative remunerative imperative operative cooperative vituperative corroborative decorative commemorative evaporative restorative narrative penetrative administrative demonstrative illustrative curative figurative accusative vegetative interpretative recitative meditative imitative authoritative consultative augmentative argumentative representative tentative sustentative portative mutative putative derivative preservative conservative laxative fixative

active reactive putrefactive inactive coactive radioactive counteractive abstractive attractive unattractive defective effective ineffective infective objective subjective adjective elective reflective intellective collective connective respective irrespective prospective retrospective introspective perspective corrective detective protective invective vindictive fictive afflictive restrictive distinctive instinctive subjunctive conjunctive disjunctive deductive seductive inductive conductive productive reproductive unproductive obstructive destructive instructive constructive depletive expletive secretive additive fugitive primitive genitive lenitive definitive infinitive punitive nutritive inquisitive transitive sensitive oversensitive positive competitive intuitive substantive attentive inattentive preventive inventive plaintive appointive

motive emotive locomotive electromotive votive captive adaptive deceptive receptive perceptive imperceptive descriptive prescriptive presumptive consumptive adoptive eruptive corruptive disruptive assertive abortive sportive furtive festive suggestive digestive restive costive exhaustive retributive contributive distributive consecutive executive diminutive constitutive vive revive survive reflexive calve halve salve valve bivalve univalve delve shelve twelve solve absolve resolve dissolve evolve devolve revolve involve

ove above cove alcove dove turtledove hove shove love clove truelove glove foxglove ladylove move remove behoove groove rove drove grove mangrove shrove throve prove reprove improve approve disapprove disprove trove strove stove wove unwove carve starve nerve innerve unnerve serve observe deserve reserve preserve conserve disserve verve swerve curve mauve

awe awe overawe ewe owe axe pickaxe deluxe aye bye goodbye dye eye deadeye redeye fisheye sockeye buckeye pinkeye walleye shuteye oxeye lye rye daze sleaze faze gaze stargaze haze kamikaze laze blaze ablaze glaze maze amaze raze braze craze graze wheeze sneeze breeze freeze refreeze unfreeze squeeze tweeze frieze trapeze

ze baize archaize maize italicize criticize faradize hybridize fluidize oxidize merchandize aggrandize methodize iodize anodize jeopardize seize elegize apologize eulogize energize catechize apostrophize sympathize focalize localize vocalize scandalize idealize realize legalize specialize materialize alkalize canalize penalize signalize finalize nationalize sectionalize mineralize moralize demoralize centralize neutralize vitalize tantalize brutalize equalize visualize spiritualize sexualize evangelize novelize mobilize volatilize fertilize utilize tranquilize civilize crystallize idolize monopolize formulize stylize macadamize itemize systemize minimize victimize legitimize optimize maximize economize atomize urbanize vulcanize organize disorganize total womanize humanize galvanize cognize recognize feminize scrutinize solemnize tyrannize agonize antagonize ionize lionize unionize revolutionize colonize demonize simonize harmonize canonize caponize patronize fraternize eternize immunize vulgarize familiarize polarize formularize popularize summarize notarize etherize polymerize characterize mischaracterize catheterize pulverize satirize odorize deodorize theorize aphorize authorize valorize memorize vaporize motorize prize apprize cicatrize size emphasize midsize resize downsize capsize oversize assize pintsize outsize dramatize schematize systematize stigmatize acclimatize poetize digitize sanitize unitize narcotize baptize peptize amortize deputize soliloquize bonze bronze doze bulldoze gloze ooze booze schmooze snooze froze unfroze furze gauze dialyze analyze paralyze catalyze

6. WORDS ENDING IN LETTER - F

af deaf sheaf leaf longleaf interleaf overleaf flyleaf pilaf oaf loaf meatloaf beef reef chef fief chief kerchief neckerchief handkerchief mischief thief belief unbelief disbelief relief brief debrief grief clef ref

ff gaff chaff raff riffraff staff pikestaff flagstaff distaff quaff biff whiff skiff cliff bailiff miff sniff spiff riff tariff midriff sheriff hippogriff tiff caitiff plaintiff pontiff stiff mastiff off scoff doff leadoff handoff standoff sendoff tradeoff takeoff kickoff knockoff falloff turnoff runoff setoff liftoff castoff blastoff cutoff shutoff showoff layoff playoff payoff buff rebuff cuff handcuff scuff duff guff huff chuff bluff fluff muff earmuff snuff puff ruff scruff dandruff gruff tuff stuff dyestuff

if waif coif serif massif aperitif motif leitmotif calf mooncalf half behalf elf shelf bookshelf pelf self oneself himself herself yourself itself thyself myself golf wolf werewolf gulf engulf hereof thereof whereof goof hoof aloof poof spoof roof sunroof proof reproof waterproof disproof woof barf scarf wharf dwarf serf scurf surf windsurf turf pouf

7. WORDS ENDING IN LETTER - G

ag bag fleabag feedbag handbag sandbag windbag nosebag ragbag workbag mailbag scumbag beanbag moneybag fag gag lollygag hag shag jag lag flag slag gulag nag snag rag brag crag drag washrag dishrag sag tag nametag retag ragtag stag wag scalawag wigwag swag zigzag beg keg muskeg leg foreleg dogleg bootleg nutmeg peg egg mahjongg

ig big dig shindig fig gig whirligig jig pig rig brig unrig prig sprig trig zaftig wig bigwig periwig earwig swig twig

ang bang shebang dang fang gang hang overhang clang slang pang rang boomerang prang sprang sang tang mustang twang yang ginseng

bing scabbing dabbing gabbing jabbing blabbing nabbing crabbing grabbing tabbing stabbing swabbing webbing fibbing ribbing cribbing bobbing fobbing jobbing lobbing mobbing hobnobbing robbing throbbing sobbing dubbing clubbing flubbing snubbing rubbing scrubbing drubbing grubbing subbing stubbing imbibing bribing scribing ascribing subscribing describing circumscribing inscribing in enrobing probing

cing acing facing defacing effacing surfacing enlacing unlacing solacing placing replacing displacing misplacing interlacing grimacing menacing spacing racing bracing embracing gracing disgracing tracing retracing fleecing piecing icing dicing deicing sufficing sacrificing policing splicing slicing rejoicing voicing invoicing pricing enticing noticing juicing sluicing dancing chancing enhancing lancing balancing overbalancing glancing financing prancing entrancing outdistancing advancing fencing inconveniencing experiencing silencing commencing recommencing influencing mincing evincing convincing wincing bouncing jouncing denouncing renouncing announcing pronouncing pouncing piercing transpiercing amercing coercing forcing enforcing reinforcing acquiescing coalescing deliquescing effervescing saucing adducing educing deducing reducing seducing inducing conducing producing reproducing introducing sprucing

ding
ding barricading unfading jading blockading unlading pomading promenading serenading cannonading spading parading abrading masquerading degrading crusading persuading evading invading pervading gadding cladding madding padding wadding bedding shedding sledding wedding bidding forbidding outbidding kidding skidding ridding plodding nodding prodding budding scudding thudding mudding pudding studding ceding acceding receding preceding seceding interceding unheeding superseding abiding deciding coinciding confiding eliding gliding deriding priding overriding striding siding subsiding presiding tiding betiding dividing subdividing providing unyielding shipbuilding landholding notwithstanding unoffending unending heartrending unpretending bookbinding faultfinding foreboding decoding encoding exploding eroding corroding including concluding excluding eluding deluding alluding denuding obtruding intruding protruding exuding being nonbeing unseeing farseeing chafing strafing vouchsafing knifing

ging
aging caging engaging disengaging mortgaging triaging pillaging damaging imaging rummaging managing

paging garaging disparaging enraging foraging encouraging discouraging envisaging advantaging assuaging ravaging savaging voyaging cadging edging hedging fledging pledging acknowledging dredging wedging ridging bridging abridging dodging lodging dislodging budging fudging judging misjudging smudging nudging drudging grudging trudging alleging reneging bagging fagging gagging shagging lagging flagging unflagging nagging snagging ragging bragging dragging sagging tagging wagging begging legging pegging digging jigging pigging rigging trigging swigging twigging bogging dogging fogging pettifogging jogging logging clogging flogging slogging togging bugging humbugging hugging chugging lugging plugging slugging drugging shrugging tugging obliging disobliging bulging indulging unchanging interchanging exchanging flanging arranging rearranging disarranging challenging avenging revenging hinging cringing fringing infringing sponging plunging lounging barging charging discharging enlarging merging emerging verging diverging converging forging gorging urging scourging purging surging gauging deluging gouging rouging

hing	aching caching unflinching douching re thing scathing seething something writhing tithing underclothing nothing farthing plaything scything anything everything

king	king baking caking faking shaking slaking making peacemaking shoemaking remaking matchmaking bookmaking unmaking haymaking snaking raking

braking forsaking taking betaking retaking partaking undertaking overtaking staking mistaking painstaking quaking waking awaking bivouacking trafficking frolicking mimicking bloodsucking eking biking hiking liking striking trekking unblinking choking joking smoking poking stroking stoking evoking revoking invoking provoking unyoking hardworking burking rebuking nuking puking

ling ling scaling haling inhaling whaling exhaling impaling staling waling cabling enabling tabling stabling babbling dabbling gabbling scrabbling grabbling squabbling pebbling dibbling nibbling scribbling quibbling bobbling cobbling gobbling hobbling wobbling bubbling enfeebling trebling sibling ambling gambling shambling rambling scrambling trembling resembling assembling dissembling bumbling fumbling humbling jumbling mumbling rumbling crumbling grumbling tumbling stumbling ennobling garbling marbling warbling burbling doubling redoubling troubling cling circling encircling muscling cycling ladling cradling addling paddling straddling saddling waddling swaddling meddling intermeddling peddling diddling fiddling middling piddling riddling twiddling coddling toddling cuddling fuddling huddling muddling wheedling needling seedling idling bridling sidling candling dandling handling kindling enkindling spindling dwindling swindling fondling bundling trundling codling doodling girdling curdling hurdling dawdling sideling traveling unfeeling changeling hireling starveling fling baffling raffling waffling piffling riffling scuffling shuffling muffling snuffling ruffling rifling trifling stifling haggling straggling waggling giggling jiggling niggling sniggling wriggling wiggling boggling goggling joggling toggling juggling smuggling struggling inveigling angling dangling gangling jangling mangling strangling wrangling tangling entangling disentangling wangling shingling jingling mingling commingling intermingling singling tingling bungling ogling gargling burgling gurgling unfailing unavailing countervailing reconciling defiling whiling smiling piling riling ensiling reviling exiling weakling cackling crackling tackling heckling speckling pickling prickling trickling tickling buckling swashbuckling duckling chuckling knuckling suckling rankling inkling sprinkling besprinkling wrinkling tinkling twinkling darkling sparkling

lling rebelling excelling gelling repelling impelling compelling propelling dispelling expelling quarrelling storytelling fuelling unwilling patrolling controlling annulling weanling holing cajoling resoling sapling stapling tripling stripling trampling sampling dimpling dumpling rumpling crumpling peopling dappling grappling rippling crippling tippling toppling purpling coupling scrupling quintupling darling yearling starling sterling sling brisling quisling gosling nursling hassling tussling tousling beetling titling entitling scantling mantling gentling footling startling chortling hurtling castling nestling wrestling whistling bristling jostling bustling hustling rustling battling rattling prattling tattling fettling nettling settling whittling bottling mottling throttling scuttling caterwauling ridiculing ruling overruling grayling styling dazzling embezzling fizzling drizzling frizzling sizzling guzzling muzzling nuzzling puzzling

ming defaming inflaming renaming framing scheming chiming liming timing scamming damming hamming shamming whamming jamming lamming slamming ramming cramming hemming lemming stemming dimming shimming skimming slimming rimming brimming trimming swimming glomming bumming gumming humming chumming slumming drumming thrumming strumming summing coming becoming unbecoming forthcoming welcoming incoming oncoming upcoming overcoming shortcoming homing chroming nonconforming fuming inhuming exhuming illuming resuming presuming consuming assuming unassuming rhyming

ning

unmeaning profaning craning unenlightening disheartening intervening undesigning uncomplaining combining seining defining refining confining imagining declining reclining inclining disinclining relining disciplining outlining bylining mining examining undermining determining illumining opining divining intertwining banning canning scanning fanning planning manning unmanning panning spanning tanning kenning penning dinning ginning beginning chinning shinning thinning skinning pinning spinning grinning sinning tinning winning twinning donning cunning dunning funning gunning shunning punning running outrunning stunning boning condoning telephoning unquestioning postponing droning atoning intoning stoning zoning rezoning undiscerning lightning communing pruning attuning doing wrongdoing going seagoing thoroughgoing ongoing easygoing

ping

ping aping escaping shaping japing draping housekeeping bookkeeping wiping swiping doping eloping interloping roping groping capping gapping happing chapping whapping lapping clapping flapping overlapping slapping mapping napping kidnapping snapping rapping crapping trapping entrapping strapping wrapping unwrapping sapping tapping swapping yapping zapping pepping prepping stepping overstepping dipping chipping shipping worshipping whipping skipping blipping clipping flipping slipping nipping snipping ripping dripping gripping tripping stripping outstripping sipping tipping quipping equipping yipping zipping bopping copping hopping chopping shopping whopping lopping clopping flopping plopping slopping mopping popping cropping dropping eavesdropping propping sopping topping stopping upping cupping supping gypping trouping typing retyping electrotyping

ring

ring uncaring daring childbearing seafaring haring

sharing blaring declaring flaring glaring snaring ensnaring preparing comparing unsparing raring squaring bewaring bring massacring interfering adhering inhering cohering overmastering unwavering revering persevering euchring hiring rehiring admiring bemiring umpiring aspiring respiring transpiring inspiring uninspiring conspiring perspiring expiring desiring tiring retiring untiring attiring acquiring requiring inquiring squiring wiring rewiring bullring boring encoring scoring underscoring adoring shoring whoring deploring imploring exploring ignoring snoring poring storing restoring spring offspring mainspring upspring dayspring barring unbarring scarring earring jarring marring sparring tarring starring warring deferring referring preferring inferring conferring transferring herring unerring disinterring averring stirring bestirring occurring recurring incurring furring blurring slurring spurring string restring latchstring hamstring unstring heartstring bowstring securing manicuring procuring during enduring figuring prefiguring abjuring adjuring injuring conjuring luring alluring immuring co inuring measuring ensuring insuring assuring reassuring featuring maturing manufacturing conjecturing lecturing picturing puncturing culturing venturing adventuring capturing torturing pasturing posturing suturing wring gyring

sing sing debasing casing encasing incasing uncasing easing ceasing unceasing releasing unpleasing displeasing appeasing creasing decreasing increasing greasing chasing purchasing repurchasing phasing phrasing paraphrasing raising braising praising incising exercising exorcising excising merchandising demising remising premising promising compromising uncompromising unpromising surmising noising despising rising arising comprising apprising enterprising surprising uprising advertising mortising disguising bruising cruising advising devising revising repulsing avulsing condensing dispensing sensing hosing losing closing enclosing inclosing unclosing disclosing choosing noosing posing deposing imposing unimposing decomposing proposing opposing supposing presupposing interposing purposing disposing predisposing transposing elapsing relapsing traipsing dispersing interspersing traversing conversing horsing reimbursing nursing coursing discoursing gassing unprepossessing intercrossing using causing pausing abusing accusing excusing reusing fusing defusing refusing effusing diffusing suffusing infusing confusing interfusing bemusing dousing housing chousing warehousing lousing blousing espousing rousing arousing carousing grousing perusing misusing drowsing

| ting |

ting abating debating rebating vacating deprecating syllabicating eradicating indicating vindicating complicating supplicating communicating excommunicating fabricating lubricating extricating authenticating intoxicating truncating suffocating locating reciprocating advocating confiscating dating sedating antedating elucidating consolidating intimidating dilapidating accommodating unaccommodating updating ideating permeating delineating creating procreating nauseating propagating legating negating aggregating congregating investigating instigating navigating interrogating objurgating conjugating emaciating depreciating appreciating officiating annunciating associating dissociating excruciating radiating irradiating repudiating retaliating conciliating humiliating foliating expiating inebriating striating expatiating ingratiating satiating vitiating aviating obviating deviating undeviating alleviating abbreviating ablating elating relating inflating dilating annihilating assimilating ventilating vacillating oscillating scintillating violating desolating insolating contemplating translating perambulating ejaculating speculating articulating gesticulating calculating uncalculating miscalculating inoculating circulating osculating stridulating undulating coagulating regulating simulating dissimulating stimulating formulating accumulating manipulating depopulating insulating congratulating expostulating amalgamating acclimating animating reanimating intimating estimating approximating emanating alienating stagnating impregnating designating vaccinating fascinating hallucinating subordinating originating disseminating incriminating discriminating culminating fulminating dominating predominating denominating germinating terminating illuminating ruminating indoctrinating procrastinating donating personating impersonating detonating alternating anticipating participating emancipating dissipating pupating exhilarating separating celebrating vibrating adumbrating crating desecrating consecrating dehydrating aerating berating liberating deliberating reverberating lacerating ulcerating moderating exaggerating refrigerating accelerating enumerating generating degenerating regenerating venerating incinerating itinerating operating exasperating vituperating commiserating obliterating transliterating adulterating disintegrating pirating orating corroborating decorating perforating invigorating ameliorating deteriorating commemorating evaporating incorporating narrating penetrating concentrating demonstrating remonstrating prostrating illustrating suppurating gyrating compensating dictating hebetating vegetating meditating agitating cogitating facilitating imitating precipitating palpitating irritating hesitating unhesitating nictitating annotating rotating devastating reinstating overstating mutating graduating extenuating insinuating equating infatuating actuating punctuating fluctuating accentuating excavating aggravating elevating salivating cultivating captivating renovating innovating enervating fixating undoubting unreflecting unsuspecting indicting deleting depleting completing competing prizefighting citing reciting inciting exciting igniting disuniting typewriting underwriting inviting unrelenting fingerprinting emoting demoting promoting denoting quoting voting devoting sting everlasting tasting uninteresting unresisting

tting chatting blatting flatting platting patting ratting tatting squatting swatting betting abetting getting begetting forgetting whetting jetting letting bloodletting petting retting fretting regretting besetting offsetting upsetting stetting pirouetting coquetting vetting wetting fitting befitting unbefitting refitting hitting shitting flitting splitting slitting submitting admitting emitting remitting unremitting committing omitting permitting intermitting transmitting manumitting knitting pitting spitting gritting sitting quitting acquitting witting unwitting twitting dotting jotting blotting clotting plotting slotting knotting potting spotting rotting trotting totting abutting cutting gutting shutting jutting glutting smutting rutting strutting

uting contributing distributing attributing prosecuting persecuting executing refuting confuting saluting eluting fluting diluting polluting commuting comminuting deputing reputing imputing computing disputing substituting instituting constituting

imbuing rescuing miscuing subduing enduing queuing leaguing plaguing intriguing fatiguing haranguing tonguing cataloguing colloguing proroguing arguing valuing bluing gluing ungluing sluing continuing piquing ruing imbruing accruing truing construing suing ensuing pursuing issuing

ving

caving heaving sheaving leaving cleaving weaving interweaving having behaving misbehaving shaving slaving enslaving paving raving braving craving engraving depraving saving staving waving peeving thieving believing unbelieving disbelieving relieving grieving reprieving retrieving sieving waiving diving deceiving undeceiving receiving conceiving perceiving giving forgiving unforgiving misgiving thanksgiving jiving skiving living reliving riving driving deriving shriving thriving depriving arriving contriving striving reviving surviving calving halving salving delving shelving solving absolving resolving dissolving evolving devolving revolving involving coving shoving loving gloving unloving moving removing unmoving grooving roving proving reproving approving disapproving disproving carving starving nerving unnerving serving observing deserving undeserving reserving preserving conserving swerving unswerving curving revving

wing-zing

wing awing redwing lacewing bitewing owing lapwing swing upswing batwing leftwing waxwing axing dying speechifying exemplifying electrifying unsatisfying lying belying highflying underlying outlying preoccupying unvarying tying retying unpitying untying vying zing dazing fazing gazing hazing lazing blazing glazing amazing razing brazing crazing grazing wheezing sneezing breezing freezing squeezing tweezing archaizing italicizing criticizing oxidizing iodizing jeopardizing seizing apologizing energizing apostrophizing philosophizing sympathizing scandalizing idealizing realizing memorializing nationalizing generalizing moralizing neutralizing tantalizing equalizing volatilizing fertilizing utilizing tranquilizing crystallizing symbolizing formulizing macadamizing systemizing legitimizing vulcanizing organizing reorganizing christianizing humanizing recognizing feminizing scrutinizing tyrannizing agonizing ionizing colonizing harmonizing patronizing fraternizing vulgarizing polarizing particularizing formularizing mesmerizing characterizing catheterizing cauterizing theorizing allegorizing authorizing memorizing temporizing factorizing prizing sizing emphasizing resizing dramatizing systematizing poetizing appetizing narcotizing bronzing dozing glozing oozing boozing snoozing analyzing paralyzing quizzing

ong bong dong gong dugong thong diphthong mahjong long along tagalong oblong headlong belong sidelong lifelong livelong weeklong oolong prolong yearlong overlong furlong daylong among pong sarong throng prong strong headstrong wrong song birdsong singsong evensong tong

ung bung dung hung overhung lung clung flung slung young rung sprung strung hamstrung unstrung wrung sung unsung shantung stung swung

og bog cog dog firedog hangdog watchdog chilidog bulldog lapdog sheepdog underdog waterdog hotdog fog befog defog pettifog agog hog quahog sandhog hedgehog warthog jog log dialog analog catalog clog unclog flog epilog backlog prolog waterlog slog smog antismog eggnog frog bullfrog leapfrog grog tog polliwog pollywog erg berg iceberg burg bug bedbug debug firebug stinkbug humbug ladybug dug hug chug thug jug lug chugalug plug fireplug unplug earplug slug mug smug snug pug rug drug shrug tug

8. WORDS ENDING IN LETTER - H

ah bah verandah obeah yeah shah pariah messiah rajah hallelujah hookah blah mullah amah nah mynah chutzpah rah menorah torah hurrah tussah cheetah halvah mitzvah ayah mezuzah huzzah

ach each beach leach bleach peach impeach reach breach preach overreach outreach teach mach stomach spinach coach stagecoach poach roach broach encroach cockroach reproach approach detach attach reattach beech leech speech breech screech beseech cromlech biotech

ich which lich rich enrich ostrich sandwich belch squelch filch zilch gulch mulch blanch ranch branch stanch bench workbench blench clench unclench drench trench retrench entrench wrench stench quench wench inch cinch finch goldfinch chaffinch bullfinch chinch clinch flinch pinch winch conch haunch launch paunch staunch bunch hunch lunch munch punch keypunch brunch crunch scrunch lynch synch

och loch hooch mooch smooch pooch brooch epoch arch search research oligarch patriarch larch march monarch parch overarch tetrarch starch perch birch smirch besmirch scorch porch torch church lurch kirsch borsch kitsch putsch batch catch hatch thatch nuthatch latch klatch unlatch potlatch match rematch overmatch mismatch outmatch snatch patch dispatch scratch watch swatch etch fetch ketch sketch retch stretch homestretch wretch vetch itch bitch ditch hitch unhitch glitch snitch pitch stitch witch bewitch switch twitch botch scotch blotch splotch notch topnotch crotch hutch clutch smutch crutch

uch debauch much insomuch overmuch forasmuch eunuch ouch couch slouch pouch crouch grouch touch retouch vouch avouch such nonesuch diptych triptych

gh sleigh neigh inveigh weigh reweigh outweigh high thigh nigh sigh burgh ugh laugh bough cough dough though although plough furlough slough enough rough through borough thorough trough sough tough pharaoh ooh pooh

ph seraph graph paragraph telegraph digraph epigraph ideograph cardiograph thermograph phonograph monograph chronograph barograph hectograph pantograph micro photograph cryptograph autograph epitaph cenotaph aleph caliph sylph oomph humph triumph lymph nymph morph dimorph glyph catarrh myrrh

ash ash bash abash calabash cash dash slapdash balderdash leash unleash gash hash rehash lash calash clash eyelash flash backlash unlash plash whiplash splash slash goulash mash mishmash smash gnash rash brash crash thrash trash sash succotash potash stash quash squash wash awash rewash whitewash eyewash hogwash backwash swash baksheesh flesh mesh enmesh fresh afresh refresh thresh

ish nebbish snobbish rubbish furbish dish radish faddish reddish cloddish childish blandish outlandish brandish fiendish modish nerdish prudish fish oafish toadfish goldfish sandfish codfish swordfish globefish candlefish cuttlefish bonefish whitefish bluefish raffish offish hagfish lungfish dogfish weakfish rockfish monkfish elfish selfish unselfish sailfish devilfish shellfish wolfish sunfish garfish starfish dwarfish butterfish silverfish catfish flatfish crawfish sawfish blowfish crayfish jellyfish waggish piggish priggish hoggish thuggish sluggish longish youngish largish roughish hashish whish freakish rakish blackish brackish sickish puckish prankish pinkish monkish bookish darkish hawkish mawkish establish reestablish disestablish publish republish relish disrelish devilish ticklish smallish tallish embellish hellish bullish abolish demolish foolish polish accomplish purplish girlish churlish mulish ghoulish owlish stylish squeamish famish blemish warmish skirmish banish womanish vanish greenish heathenish finish refinish diminish swinish knish clannish mannish donnish hunnish monish admonish astonish garnish tarnish varnish burnish furnish punish clownish brownish jingoish apish sheepish dampish impish lumpish plumpish frumpish popish snappish foppish waspish bearish garish parish gibberish cherish perish waterish feverish impoverish fairish whorish boorish flourish nourish latish sweetish fetish whitish is coltish doltish fattish pettish coquettish skittish sluttish loutish brutish anguish languish distinguish extinguish roguish voguish bluish cliquish vanquish relinquish squish lavish slavish knavish ravish peevish thievish dervish wish shrewish yellowish swish grayish babyish toadyish boyish puppyish pixyish

osh-ush | kibosh gosh josh galosh slosh nosh whoosh swoosh posh frosh mackintosh harsh marsh bush rosebush ambush gush hush shush lush blush flush plush slush mush push rush brush sagebrush nailbrush underbrush airbrush hairbrush crush thrush bulrush inrush onrush

ath-ith | bath birdbath death heath sheath beneath underneath breath wreath bequeath hath lath math aftermath polymath oath loath path osteopath warpath footpath towpath bypath wrath swath breadth handbreadth hairbreadth hundredth width thousandth teeth eyeteeth fiftieth eightieth seventieth twentieth thirtieth fortieth sixtieth shibboleth fifth twelfth length wavelength strength eighth faith unfaith wraith kith megalith eolith monolith smith goldsmith blacksmith locksmith tinsmith gunsmith zenith pith with herewith therewith wherewith forthwith

lth-uh

health stealth wealth commonwealth filth warmth nth amaranth nineteenth fifteenth eighteenth seventeenth thirteenth fourteenth sixteenth tenth eleventh seventh hyacinth plinth ninth labyrinth millionth month midmonth twelvemonth both cloth broadcloth tablecloth cerecloth sackcloth oilcloth sloth moth behemoth mammoth booth tollbooth smooth sooth tooth eyetooth broth froth toroth troth betroth wroth mitzvoth matzoth depth earth dearth hearth unearth berth birth childbirth rebirth stillbirth afterbirth firth girth mirth forth henceforth thenceforth north worth pennyworth fourth sleuth azimuth bismuth couth uncouth mouth badmouth vermouth south youth truth untruth mistruth growth undergrowth outgrowth sixth myth huh

9. WORDS ENDING IN LETTER - I

i

lanai samurai bonsai syllabi kohlrabi rabbi alibi nimbi rhombi thrombi obi incubi abaci umbilici foci loci menisci midi caducei lei nuclei sansei glutei esophagi magi fungi yogi chi hibachi gnocchi chichi bronchi litchi phi sushi acanthi radii kanji basenji shoji khaki sukiyaki teriyaki dashiki ski kabuki saluki alkali deli chili nautili phalli vermicelli bacilli piccalilli emboli broccoli nucleoli alveoli gladioli ravioli stimuli cumuli tumuli annuli lazuli styli origami thalami salami tsunami pastrami hippopotami swami semi sashimi pa timpani tympani maharani bambini zucchini bikini mini termini martini linguini alumni jinni spumoni macaroni ciceroni rigatoni mythoi poi envoi borzoi okapi tipi scampi tempi safari tamari certiorari sari beriberi uteri daiquiri posteriori pylori signori yakitori cirri potpourri thesauri papyri quasi nisi virtuosi tarsi narcissi colossi coati literati cacti spermaceti yeti graffiti wapiti anti concerti confetti agouti ennui nevi kiwi maxi taxi

10. WORDS ENDING IN LETTER - K

ak-eck
beak grosbeak leak bleak sneak peak speak bespeak misspeak newspeak break heartbreak outbreak daybreak creak freak streak wreak teak steak beefsteak squeak weak tweak flak kulak oak cloak uncloak croak soak presoak anorak yak kayak back aback feedback holdback hardback tieback zwieback stickleback comeback bareback horseback halfback wingback hogback hunchback kickback tailback callback fallback rollback fullback pullback runback snapback humpback leatherback canvasback mossback fatback setback wetback fastback cutback outback drawback skewback playback payback swayback buyback hack shack whack jack highjack hijack blackjack flapjack slapjack bootjack skyjack lack black clack flack slack smack knack knickknack snack pack mudpack repack backpack unpack rack tamarack crack gimcrack rickrack bookrack barrack track wrack hayrack sack packsack rucksack woolsack ransack knapsack tack hardtack ticktack stack smokestack haystack attack quack thwack beck deck bedeck sundeck heck check recheck hatcheck paycheck fleck neck redneck bottleneck crewneck peck henpeck kopeck speck flyspeck wreck shipwreck

ick
dick hick chick thick kick sidekick dropkick lick click flick rollick slick bootlick cowlick gimmick nick snick pick handpick spick brick redbrick crick limerick maverick prick pinprick derrick trick sick seasick homesick lovesick carsick airsick tick shtick politick stick fiddlestick candlestick broomstick drumstick nonstick slapstick dipstick lipstick joystick quick wick bailiwick

ock-ik
bock cock peacock woodcock shuttlecock gamecock

stopcock weathercock petcock dock haddock paddock undock burdock hock chock shock hollyhock jock lock block unblock clock deadlock headlock padlock wedlock gridlock forelock flock schlock antilock picklock hillock bullock hemlock unlock gunlock oarlock warlock fetlock flintlock rowlock mock hammock hummock smock nock knock pock rock crock bedrock frock defrock unfrock shamrock sock windsock cassock hassock tussock stock restock laughingstock alpenstock overstock rootstock mattock buttock buck megabuck roebuck sawbuck duck chuck upchuck shuck luck cluck pluck potluck muck amuck puck truck struck moonstruck thunderstruck suck tuck stuck unstuck yuck geek cheek leek sleek meek peek reek creek seek week midweek workweek shriek trek sheik nudnik peacenik beatnik sputnik batik

lk balk chalk talk shoptalk stalk eyestalk leafstalk outtalk walk sidewalk cakewalk moonwalk catwalk jaywalk skywalk elk whelk ilk bilk milk foremilk buttermilk soymilk silk folk gentlefolk kinfolk kinsfolk townsfolk yolk caulk bulk hulk skulk sulk bank databank sandbank cloudbank mountebank embank dank hank shank thank lank blank clank flank outflank plank spank rank crank drank frank shrank prank outrank sank tank antitank stank swank yank ink fink chink think bethink rethink outthink kink skink link blink clink unlink bobolink plink slink mink oink pink rink brink drink shrink prink sink stink wink hoodwink eyewink conk honk monk bunk debunk dunk funk gunk hunk chunk junk skunk clunk flunk plunk slunk chipmunk punk spunk drunk shrunk trunk sunk stunk

ok steenbok gemsbok amok book handbook wordbook studbook guidebook rebook casebook notebook bluebook songbook logbook sketchbook bankbook cookbook workbook hymnbook hornbook chapbook yearbook overbook passbook pocketbook textbook daybook copybook cook precook overcook gook hook fishhook billhook unhook shook pothook kook look overlook outlook nook inglenook schnook spook rook brook crook forsook took betook retook partook undertook overtook mistook kapok wok

rk ark bark debark shagbark embark disembark tanbark dark hark shark lark titlark skylark mark landmark trademark tidemark remark birthmark pockmark bookmark hallmark earmark watermark postmark nark park ballpark spark stark quark aardvark bulwark hauberk jerk clerk perk berserk irk dirk shirk smirk quirk cork uncork dork fork pitchfork pork stork work beadwork headwork roadwork handwork groundwork woodwork lacework piecework latticework lifework needlework trestlework framework homework stonework rework firework wirework casework housework legwork patchwork meshwork earthwork handiwork hackwork brickwork clockwork rockwork wheelwork millwork teamwork openwork ironwork wickerwork overwork guesswork seatwork ductwork basketwork network cabinetwork fretwork footwork artwork breastwork outwork waxwork bodywork busywork lurk murk

sk ask bask cask flask mask damask unmask task subtask desk copydesk disk whisk obelisk basilisk risk tamarisk brisk asterisk frisk kiosk dusk husk cornhusk mollusk musk tusk auk mukluk gawk hawk tomahawk goshawk squawk

11. WORDS ENDING IN LETTER - L

bal cannibal scribal tribal cymbal global herbal verbal zodiacal maniacal demoniacal paradisiacal decal fecal laical pharisaical cubical farcical radical medical juridical methodical periodical pontifical

cal magical logical genealogical mineralogical illogical ideological geological theological psychological morphological pathological mythological biological bacteriological physiological etymological zoological meteorological eschatological herpetological tautological surgical liturgical monarchical hierarchical psychical graphical geographical or biographical ethnographical typographical philosophical ethical mythical biblical cyclical evangelical helical umbilical diabolical symbolical dynamical chemical rhythmical inimical comical economical astronomical anatomical mechanical photomechanical botanical ecumenical technical ethnical rabbinical finical clinical tyrannical conical canonical ironical cynical stoical apical epical tropical subtropical topical typical atypical cylindrical spherical hemispherical clerical chimerical numerical hysterical empirical satirical allegorical categorical metaphorical oratorical rhetorical historical theatrical electrical metrical symmetrical unsymmetrical geometrical lyrical lackadaisical whimsical nonsensical classical musical unmusical physical metaphysical psychophysical mathematical problematical systematical enigmatical grammatical ungrammatical fanatical piratical didactical practical tactical alphabetical pathetical hypothetical arithmetical poetical heretical theoretical political critical diacritical hypocritical hypercritical identical skeptical elliptical optical vertical cortical ecclesiastical pa fantastical logistical sophistical egotistical mystical nautical pharmaceutical cervical lexical paradoxical quizzical focal bifocal trifocal local reciprocal vocal univocal equivocal unequivocal unvocal rascal mescal fiscal ducal

dal medal pedal bipedal regicidal homicidal parricidal patricidal fratricidal suicidal pyramidal rhomboidal colloidal bridal tidal scandal sandal vandal modal bimodal nodal caudal feudal

eal-hal conceal deal ideal ordeal misdeal congeal pharyngeal laryngeal heal tracheal wheal meal piecemeal fishmeal cornmeal oatmeal hymeneal cochineal lineal pineal anneal peritoneal corneal peal repeal appeal real cereal sidereal ethereal venereal funereal unreal boreal arboreal corporeal incorporeal surreal empyreal seal reseal unseal teal lacteal steal squeal veal reveal weal zeal offal gal legal illegal regal prodigal madrigal fungal fugal centrifugal conjugal frugal epochal patriarchal paschal triumphal apocryphal marshal lethal zenithal withal wherewithal betrothal narwhal

ial labial bilabial adverbial proverbial facial glacial racial biracial special especial judicial prejudicial beneficial official unofficial artificial superficial financial provincial uncial social asocial antisocial commercial crucial dial radial medial remedial redial gerundial sundial cordial primordial misdial collegial brachial bronchial parochial phial epithelial filial familial binomial trinomial monomial polynomial cranial denial genial congenial uncongenial menial venial finial biennial millennial quadrennial perennial colonial ceremonial matrimonial patrimonial testimonial baronial espial marsupial malarial filarial secretarial aerial imperial serial material immaterial bacterial arterial ministerial ambassadorial memorial immemorial armorial manorial piscatorial accusatorial dictatorial equatorial factorial pictorial editorial territorial inquisitorial tutorial uxorial trial retrial pretrial terrestrial mistrial industrial burial reburial mercurial ambrosial controversial palatial spatial equinoctial initial interstitial substantial insubstantial unsubstantial circumstantial credential confidential presidential providential prudential tangential pestilential exponential deferential preferential differential inferential reverential essential inessential nonessential unessential penitential potential influential consequential inconsequential nuptial martial partial impartial inertial bestial celestial colloquial vial gavial trivial convivial jovial fluvial postdiluvial alluvial pluvial axial coaxial jackal

mal decimal animal minimal primal infinitesimal optimal maximal proximal mammal dermal epidermal thermal isothermal formal informal normal abnormal miasmal phantasmal dismal baptismal abysmal lachrymal

nal anal banal canal duodenal phenomenal penal renal adrenal arsenal venal signal medicinal officinal vicinal cardinal ordinal longitudinal final vaginal original aboriginal unoriginal marginal virginal synclinal seminal criminal abdominal nominal pronominal germinal terminal spinal doctrinal urinal retinal dentinal intestinal autumnal hymnal diagonal tetragonal octagonal pentagonal hexagonal orthogonal polygonal antiphonal regional occasional visional divisional provisional recessional processional confessional professional unprofessional educational ideational national international rational irrational sensational conversational gravitational fractional sectional fictional functional constructional traditional additional conditional volitional transitional prepositional intentional unintentional conventional unconventional motional emotional unemotional notional devotional exceptional optional proportional institutional constitutional hormonal coronal neuronal seasonal personal impersonal tonal atonal zonal carnal infernal supernal maternal paternal fraternal eternal internal external vernal diurnal journal nocturnal faunal tribunal communal coal charcoal foal goal shoal pal papal sepal municipal principal oedipal opal copal archiepiscopal carpal

ral

cerebral vertebral sacral dodecahedral octahedral dihedral cathedral polyhedral liberal illiberal visceral federal feral peripheral cameral bicameral ephemeral numeral general mineral funeral puerperal lateral quadrilateral equilateral collateral literal several integral sepulchral admiral spiral viral oral coral choral floral chloral moral amoral femoral immoral unmoral temporal corporal electoral pectoral doctoral clitoral pastoral littoral mayoral chaparral deferral referral corral demurral spectral central ventral astral ancestral orchestral mistral austral neutral dextral aural binaural monaural pleural neural figural augural plural mural rural commissural natural connatural unnatural supernatural preternatural architectural structural cultural agricultural floricultural horticultural scriptural unscriptural sculptural postural guttural textural flexural

sal

basal nasal phrasal appraisal reprisal sisal revisal mensal deposal proposal supposal disposal rehearsal tarsal metatarsal tars dispersal reversal universal dorsal vassal missal dismissal colossal abyssal causal refusal spousal espousal arousal carousal perusal

tal

fatal nonfatal palatal natal prenatal neonatal postnatal fractal rectal octal fetal vegetal societal parietal skeletal metal bimetal nonmetal gunmetal petal centripetal barbital orbital postorbital recital digital genital congenital coital capital occipital hospital marital requital vital consonantal placental dental accidental occidental incidental coincidental transcendental oriental mental fundamental firmamental ornamental sacramental temperamental elemental incremental fragmental segmental rudimental regimental experimental sentimental unsentimental governmental monumental instrumental hi continental rental parental quintal frontal horizontal contrapuntal sacerdotal scrotal total subtotal teetotal pivotal aortal mortal immortal portal coastal pedestal festal vestal distal postal crystal remittal committal acquittal glottal rebuttal brutal

| ual-zal | dual gradual residual individual lingual sublingual manual bimanual continual annual biannual semiannual equal unequal coequal accrual menstrual casual visual sensual consensual usual unusual actual factual tactual effectual ineffectual intellectual victual punctual unpunctual perpetual habitual ritual spiritual eventual conceptual virtual mutual textual sexual asexual bisexual upheaval naval mediaeval medieval primeval coeval gingival archival carnival rival deprival arrival corrival infinitival festival revival survival oval removal approval disapproval larval interval withdrawal eschewal renewal bestowal avowal disavowal defrayal betrayal portrayal loyal disloyal royal quetzal

| el | label mislabel rebel jezebel decibel libel corbel pedicel cancel chancel parcel excel citadel infidel roundel asphodel model remodel yodel strudel eel feel heel wheel freewheel cogwheel pinwheel flywheel keel kneel peel reel creel unreel newsreel genteel steel falafel duffel gel bagel cudgel angel archangel satchel bushel bethel brothel spaniel spiel materiel oriel nickel pumpernickel shekel

yokel snorkel parallel camel enamel caramel trammel pommel pummel calomel panel empanel impanel fontanel crenel sentinel cannel channel flannel fennel kennel personnel funnel runnel tunnel colonel grapnel shrapnel darnel charnel kernel pimpernel noel chapel lapel repel scalpel impel compel propel rappel dispel gospel expel apparel gambrel tumbrel mandrel spandrel scoundrel doggerel mackerel pickerel cockerel mongrel morel barrel carrel quarrel squirrel sorrel petrel wastrel kestrel minstrel laurel easel teasel weasel groundsel diesel chisel damsel tinsel counsel morsel passel tassel vessel mussel streusel fusel carousel muscatel boatel betel mantel lintel hotel motel cartel pastel hostel chattel duel fuel refuel sequel cruel gruel gavel navel ravel caravel gravel unravel travel bevel dishevel level sublevel revel snivel drivel shrivel swivel hovel shovel novel grovel marvel jewel bejewel newel crewel bowel embowel disembowel dowel rowel trowel towel vowel pixel hazel bezel pretzel ouzel kohl

il ail bail fail hail jail flail mail blackmail airmail nail treenail toenail hangnail doornail snail pail rail handrail derail frail grail monorail trail contrail sail headsail foresail mainsail topsail assail wassail tail bobtail swordtail detail retail horsetail dovetail wagtail pigtail ringtail hightail fishtail cocktail fantail entail pintail cottontail curtail cattail coattail rattail swallowtail yellowtail oxtail foxtail ponytail quail avail travail prevail wail bewail

gerbil codicil pencil stencil council daffodil vermeil nonpareil veil unveil sigil vigil argil mil nil oil boil gumboil parboil potboil coil recoil uncoil foil trefoil cinquefoil tinfoil airfoil moil turmoil spoil despoil roil broil embroil soil subsoil topsoil toil pupil aril fibril tendril peril imperil nostril basil utensil tonsil fossil lentil until distil pistil fauteuil tranquil jonquil cavil evil devil bedevil weevil civil uncivil anvil chervil brazil

all | all ball oddball handball hardball fireball baseball eyeball puffball goofball highball mothball kickball pinball cornball hairball sourball meatball softball spitball football fastball lowball snowball call birdcall recall overcall miscall catcall fall deadfall landfall windfall befall icefall rainfall downfall waterfall pratfall nightfall pitfall footfall snowfall gall hall catchall guildhall shall mall small pall appall overall coverall thrall enthrall tall stall forestall bookstall install squall wall seawall drywall carryall

ell | ell bell dumbbell bluebell barbell doorbell cowbell cell dell fell befell hell shell seashell bombshell cockleshell eggshell nutshell jell smell knell spell respell misspell sell resell undersell oversell outsell tell retell foretell quell well dwell indwell farewell inkwell unwell swell yell

ill | ill bill handbill duckbill hornbill razorbill playbill waybill dill fill landfill refill backfill fulfill overfill gill bluegill hill chill molehill dunghill downhill uphill shill anthill foothill kill overkill skill mill treadmill windmill sawmill pill spill rill drill mandrill frill grill shrill thrill krill trill sill doorsill windowsill till still standstill distill instill quill will goodwill freewill whippoorwill swill twill boll doll loll moll knoll poll roll scroll droll bedroll bankroll enroll reenroll unroll troll stroll payroll toll atoll bull cull scull dull full overfull gull seagull hull skull numbskull numskull lull mull null pull idyll chlorophyll

ol-rl | gambol symbol protocol glycol idol googol alcohol gasohol menthol vitriol viol frijol ethanol methanol phenol cool overcool fool school pool whirlpool vanpool carpool spool cesspool drool tool retool stool barstool footstool wool carol glycerol folderol bannerol sterol patrol petrol control sol parasol cresol creosol aerosol capitol pistol extol frivol earl pearl marl gnarl snarl ensnarl unsnarl girl schoolgirl cowgirl showgirl playgirl whirl awhirl skirl swirl twirl whorl burl curl uncurl furl unfurl hurl churl knurl purl

ul haul keelhaul overhaul maul bulbul tubful dreadful heedful needful handful mindful unmindful regardful disregardful peaceful graceful ungraceful disgraceful forceful resourceful prideful gleeful changeful vengeful revengeful wakeful baleful guileful doleful shameful blameful baneful tuneful woeful hopeful careful ireful direful easeful purposeful remorseful useful fateful hateful plateful grateful ungrateful spiteful tasteful distasteful wasteful rueful eyeful meaningful wrongful reproachful watchful bashful wishful wrathful faithful unfaithful healthful slothful mirthful mouthful youthful ruthful truthful untruthful fanciful merciful unmerciful pitiful plentiful bountiful beautiful dutiful undutiful thankful unthankful forkful skilful skillful unskillful willful soulful brimful doomful roomful armful harmful manful spleenful disdainful gainful painful sinful spoonful teaspoonful tablespoonful dessertspoonful scornful mournful capful worshipful helpful cupful earful fearful tearful jarful wonderful cheerful masterful powerful colorful glassful successful unsuccessful stressful distressful blissful doubtful tactful respectful disrespectful forgetful pocketful basketful fretful regretful delightful rightful frightful thoughtful deceitful fitful fruitful unfruitful resentful eventful uneventful artful hurtful boastful restful zestful fistful wistful lustful trustful distrustful mistrustful awful lawful unlawful sorrowful playful bellyful joyful mogul karakul annul disannul

oul

foul afoul befoul ghoul soul consul awl bawl bradawl shawl pawl brawl crawl scrawl drawl sprawl trawl yawl mewl owl bowl punchbowl washbowl fishbowl cowl scowl fowl peafowl seafowl wildfowl howl jowl growl prowl yowl sibyl ethyl methyl alkyl amyl phenyl biphenyl vinyl carbonyl aryl beryl dactyl pterodactyl acetyl butyl carboxyl hydroxyl benzyl

12. WORDS ENDING IN LETTER - M

am cam scam dam macadam madam beldam milldam quondam cofferdam beam abeam moonbeam sunbeam gleam agleam ream bream cream scream dream daydream stream downstream upstream seam inseam team steam amalgam ham graham gingham brougham sham wham jam logjam lam clam bedlam flimflam slam imam foam antifoam loam roam diazepam ram cram scram dram fluidram wolfram gram decagram diagram anagram hexagram telegram decigram milligram epigram ideogram echogram parallelogram kilogram hologram tomogram monogram sonogram program hectogram cryptogram lettergram ashram buckram marjoram pram tram balsam jetsam flotsam tam bantam wigwam swam exam yam

em diadem anadem idem tandem modem deem redeem misdeem seem teem esteem disesteem fem gem stratagem hem sachem them anthem apothem mayhem requiem emblem problem xylem phloem poem proem harem theorem item totem postmortem stem system diaphragm apothegm phlegm paradigm ohm logarithm rhythm aim claim acclaim declaim reclaim proclaim disclaim quitclaim exclaim maim misaim cherubim dim bedim him seraphim shim whim skim prelim slim denim minim rim brim scrim interim grim megrim pilgrim prim trim passim verbatim seriatim victim vim swim maxim balm embalm calm becalm realm palm napalm psalm qualm elm helm whelm overwhelm film hmm umm

om noncom intercom sitcom freedom dukedom boredom fiefdom chiefdom selfdom serfdom kingdom sheikdom officialdom seldom thralldom earldom filmdom random condom stardom martyrdom wisdom fathom whom idiom axiom shalom slalom glom whilom mom cardamom nom venom envenom boom doom foredoom loom bloom abloom handloom gloom heirloom simoom room tearoom broom clubroom headroom bedroom boardroom guardroom wardroom homeroom storeroom stateroom anteroom groom bridegroom legroom washroom mushroom bathroom cloakroom backroom sickroom darkroom workroom ballroom schoolroom poolroom sunroom taproom barroom newsroom coatroom restroom elbowroom showroom dayroom playroom zoom pompom carom from therefrom pogrom prom angstrom maelstrom besom hansom ransom transom bosom blossom tom atom diatom phantom symptom custom accustom bottom buxom

rm arm yardarm sidearm rearm firearm forearm farm harm charm alarm unarm underarm disarm warm lukewarm swarm endoderm echinoderm mesoderm ectoderm pachyderm germ isotherm perm sperm term midterm firm affirm reaffirm infirm confirm reconfirm squirm corm dorm form landform deform freeform reform waveform pr cuneiform la vermiform uniform multiform oviform inform conform microform chloroform perform transform platform norm storm windstorm thunderstorm snowstorm worm woodworm tapeworm ringworm inchworm earthworm silkworm bookworm hookworm mealworm pinworm flatworm cutworm glowworm sarcasm orgasm chasm enthusiasm neoplasm protoplasm cytoplasm pleonasm spasm phantasm

ism ism archaism snobbism cubism racism solecism cynicism stoicism lyricism fanaticism didacticism eclecticism criticism eroticism skepticism scholasticism monasticism agnosticism mysticism witticism exorcism fascism sadism nudism

deism ageism theism atheism monotheism seism pacifism dwarfism
savagism syllogism neologism catechism anarchism schism sophism
dimorphism cabalism cannibalism radicalism evangelicalism
localism vocalism idealism realism legalism provincialism socialism
colonialism imperialism materialism experientialism colloquialism
animalism formalism nationalism rationalism traditionalism
emotionalism journalism liberalism literalism fatalism non dualism
individualism spiritualism conceptualism parallelism pugilism
nihilism diabolism embolism symbolism holism alcoholism
somnambulism populism botulism dynamism euphemism animism
pessimism optimism urbanism volcanism paganism organism
mechanism pianism humanism charlatanism tokenism albinism
feminism libertinism hedonism antagonism unionism creationism
monism demonism anachronism modernism communism egoism
jingoism heroism escapism tropism hydrotropism barbarism
plagiarism czarism mesmerism mannerism pauperism asterism
chrism aphorism terrorism prism tourism purism naturism futurism
bossism astigmatism dogmatism rheumatism conservatism pietism
quietism magnetism syncretism elitism obscurantism egotism
patriotism hypnotism nepotism despotism baptism autism absolutism
ventriloquism truism altruism atavism civism recidivism activism
collectivism fauvism sexism toadyism cronyism

osm　microcosm abysm cataclysm aneurysm paroxysm
meerschaum bum sebum album cum modicum colchicum
capsicum viaticum talcum locum scum sedum dumdum
memorandum addendum pudendum agendum corundum athenaeum
lyceum rheum ileum linoleum petroleum mausoleum perineum
peritoneum coliseum museum gum hum chum sorghum

ium　labium cambium columbium niobium erbium terbium

ytterbium calcium francium caladium palladium vanadium radium stadium medium tedium rubidium iridium scandium compendium indium odium rhodium plasmodium podium sodium pericardium myocardium brachium lithium nobelium mycelium helium epithelium endothelium cilium gallium thallium trillium beryllium thulium cadmium premium holmium encomium chromium fermium osmium didymium neodymium cranium geranium uranium titanium rhenium ruthenium selenium hafnium gadolinium actinium biennium millennium zirconium polonium pandemonium ammonium harmonium opium europium barium herbarium solarium samarium planetarium aquarium equilibrium opprobrium cerium bacterium delirium corium thorium emporium sanatorium auditorium scriptorium atrium yttrium curium tellurium gymnasium cesium magnesium potassium lutetium tritium effluvium alluvium

kum-num oakum bunkum hokum alum tantalum hoodlum velum glum cerebellum vellum plum peplum exemplum sugarplum slum pabulum speculum vinculum operculum pendulum coagulum phylum asylum mum chrysanthemum minimum optimum maximum laudanum tympanum duodenum plenum sphagnum magnum aluminum platinum sternum

rum-wum laburnum jejunum wampum rum arum alarum labrum candelabrum cerebrum sacrum fulcrum scrum drum kettledrum humdrum conundrum eardrum serum thrum decorum indecorum forum variorum quorum plectrum spectrum tantrum strum estrum nostrum rostrum aurum durum sum gypsum dorsum possum opossum alyssum datum petrolatum ultimatum pomatum desideratum ageratum erratum stratum substratum rectum dictum sanctum quantum momentum scrotum factotum septum frustum sputum adytum vacuum residuum ovum swum

| ym | gym pseudonym allonym homonym synonym eponym acronym metonym antonym |

13. WORDS ENDING IN LETTER - N

ban ban urban suburban turban can pecan ashcan barbican publican republican pelican pemmican oilcan cancan scan toucan sedan harridan paean bean soybean cetacean crustacean ocean dean jean lean clean unclean glean cerulean mean demean subterranean me cesarean empyrean protean quean wean fan turbofan pagan began toboggan cardigan mulligan hooligan ptarmigan slogan brogan organ afghan khan astrakhan orphan than leviathan

ian lesbian magician logician academician technician patrician electrician musician physician metaphysician mathematician theoretician politician optician radian tragedian median comedian ophidian meridian viridian obsidian custodian guardian plebeian ruffian collegian stygian me carnelian reptilian civilian bohemian isthmian simian fallopian utopian thespian barbarian abecedarian grammarian planarian sexagenarian valetudinarian riparian librarian agrarian sectarian vegetarian utilitarian humanitarian antiquarian ovarian valerian salutatorian stentorian historian pedestrian equestrian saurian elysian titian dietitian gentian tertian unchristian fustian avian antediluvian postdiluvian
clan raglan plan preplan

man man seaman shaman cabman adman headman madman freedman husbandman sandman bondman soundman yardman birdman spaceman iceman policeman sideman freeman committeeman brakeman stableman nobleman middleman rifleman gentleman lineman fireman foreman longshoreman baseman horseman caveman bagman gagman flagman ragman hangman workingman wingman frogman coachman henchman churchman watchman pitchman freshman bushman caiman packman stickman stockman milkman junkman workman wheelman hotelman mailman councilman oilman dolman patrolman penman trainman unman gunman yeoman radioman roman ottoman woman madwoman gentlewoman workwoman charwoman washerwoman airwoman kinswoman laywoman countrywoman midshipman barman lumberman alderman trencherman fisherman merman superman airman chairman doorman motorman beadsman headsman leadsman bondsman woodsman backwoodsman guardsman herdsman swordsman tradesman spokesman salesman linesman statesman talisman marksman almsman helmsman groomsman clansman kinsman gownsman townsman corpsman oarsman steersman chessman pressman batsman huntsman sportsman busman newsman boatman merchantman stuntman footman postman human subhuman inhuman superhuman lawman crewman cowman showman plowman snowman taxman layman highwayman handyman bogeyman journeyman clergyman funnyman dairyman ferryman countryman juryman jazzman

| oan-van | loan moan bemoan roan groan metazoan pan deadpan bedpan hardpan saucepan trepan dishpan marzipan sampan span wingspan dustpan ran saran bran reran foreran veteran shoran loran overran sporran outran diocesan courtesan artisan partisan tan charlatan tarlatan caftan metropolitan puritan titan sultan suntan tartan sacristan capstan rattan van caravan divan minivan sylvan cordovan wan rowan swan cyan |

| den | den deaden leaden menhaden laden broaden gladden madden sadden redden bidden unbidden forbidden hidden |

chidden ridden bedridden overridden stridden trodden downtrodden sodden sudden maiden handmaiden widen olden embolden golden beholden linden bounden wooden garden harden warden churchwarden burden unburden overburden disburden hoyden

een been sheen keen nankeen baleen colleen spleen peen careen screen green wintergreen evergreen preen tureen seen foreseen unforeseen unseen overseen teen lateen sateen nineteen preteen velveteen fifteen eighteen canteen seventeen umpteen thirteen fourteen sixteen queen between

fen-len fen deafen stiffen collagen smidgen antigen glycogen pathogen halogen fibrinogen androgen hydrogen nitrogen estrogen cryogen allergen roentgen oxygen hen peahen lichen richen kitchen roughen toughen hyphen moorhen ashen freshen then heathen lengthen strengthen smoothen earthen when lien alien mien ken weaken shaken unshaken oaken forsaken taken betaken retaken partaken undertaken overtaken mistaken waken awaken reawaken blacken slacken bracken chicken thicken stricken awestricken sicken quicken liken silken drunken shrunken sunken spoken bespoken unspoken outspoken broken unbroken heartbroken token betoken woken awoken darken hearken glen fallen befallen downfallen crestfallen pollen swollen sullen woolen stolen

men men amen seamen cyclamen foramen stamen cabmen admen headmen madmen freedmen husbandmen sandmen bondmen soundmen yardmen birdmen spacemen icemen policemen sidemen freemen brakemen noblemen middlemen riflemen gentlemen linemen firemen foremen semen basemen horsemen warehousemen cavemen bagmen gagmen flagmen ragmen hangmen workingmen wingmen frogmen coachmen henchmen churchmen watchmen pitchmen freshmen bushmen specimen regimen packmen stickmen stockmen milkmen junkmen workmen wheelmen hotelmen mailmen oilmen dolmen penmen trainmen gunmen

omen abdomen yeomen radiomen agnomen cognomen women madwomen gentlewomen forewomen washerwomen airwomen saleswomen kinswomen laywomen midshipmen barmen lumbermen aldermen fishermen mermen supermen airmen chairmen doormen motormen beadsmen headsmen leadsmen bondsmen woodsmen backwoodsmen herdsmen tradesmen salesmen linesmen statesmen marksmen almsmen helmsmen groomsmen clansmen kinsmen gownsmen townsmen corpsmen oarsmen chessmen pressmen batsmen craftsmen huntsmen sportsmen busmen newsmen boatmen selectmen stuntmen footmen postmen albumen acumen lumen rumen bitumen lawmen crewmen cowmen showmen fellowmen plowmen snowmen taxmen laymen highwaymen handymen bogeymen journeymen clergymen hymen funnymen dairymen cavalrymen ferrymen countrymen jurymen jazzmen linen

pen pen cheapen misshapen deepen pigpen ripen bullpen dampen open reopen happen sharpen aspen playpen children grandchildren brethren siren barren warren wren samisen risen arisen chosen loosen unloosen coarsen worsen lessen delicatessen

ten ten eaten beaten unbeaten browbeaten wheaten uneaten greaten threaten platen oaten paten sweeten often soften straighten heighten lighten enlighten brighten frighten tighten straiten whiten molten verboten hearten marten smarten shorten fasten refasten unfasten hasten chasten tungsten listen glisten moisten christen batten fatten flatten bitten unbitten kitten mitten smitten written handwritten typewritten rewritten unwritten gotten begotten misbegotten forgotten rotten tauten gluten

ven-zen heaven leaven haven shaven unshaven maven raven craven graven even eleven uneven seven given forgiven liven enliven driven overdriven shriven thriven striven oven coven cloven proven unproven woven rewoven interwoven flaxen waxen vixen oxen yen doyen brazen bedizen denizen citizen wizen cozen dozen frozen refrozen unfrozen mizzen

ain campaign arraign condign deign feign reign sovereign foreign align realign malign misalign benign sign design redesign resign ensign consign cosign countersign assign reassign impugn oppugn autobahn
ordain foreordain preordain disdain gain again regain bargain chain enchain unchain lain blain porcelain villain plain chaplain complain explain chamberlain overlain slain main legerdemain remain domain pain rain brain midbrain forebrain drain suzerain refrain grain engrain ingrain sprain terrain murrain train quatrain detrain retrain entrain strain restrain constrain obtain detain retain plantain maintain contain fountain mountain captain certain uncertain ascertain pertain appertain entertain curtain stain abstain sustain attain vain swain boatswain coxswain twain bin cabin bobbin nubbin woodbin thrombin hemoglobin robin dustbin niacin neomycin din paladin

ein skein mullein rein herein therein wherein checkrein casein protein stein vein fin olefin paraffin griffin coffin muffin ragamuffin puffin elfin bowfin gin pidgin begin noggin origin margin virgin chin baldachin urchin capuchin dolphin dauphin shin thin lecithin within gaijin

kin-nn kin akin bodkin ramekin munchkin manikin welkin devilkin napkin bumpkin pumpkin gherkin jerkin firkin skin lambskin kidskin moleskin wineskin doeskin foreskin calfskin pigskin buckskin sealskin oilskin woolskin coonskin sheepskin bearskin deerskin goatskin buskin catkin ptyalin goblin maudlin zeppelin javelin myelin vanillin gremlin drumlin kaolin mandolin pangolin violin lanolin poplin marlin muslin tarpaulin globulin insulin

gamin thiamin vitamin vermin albumin cumin melanin lignin tannin rennin coin join subjoin adjoin rejoin enjoin conjoin disjoin loin tenderloin sirloin purloin heroin groin ligroin quoin pin terrapin chinquapin tiepin tholepin ninepin kingpin linchpin lynchpin pushpin stickpin duckpin tenpin unpin pippin underpin hairpin spin clothespin backspin tailspin topspin hatpin mandarin saccharin heparin alizarin fibrin glycerin nitroglycerin grin chagrin aspirin florin dextrin burin sin basin moccasin tocsin resin oleoresin raisin eosin rosin myosin pepsin amylopsin assassin cousin tin gelatin keratin gratin satin pectin bulletin cretin chitin dentin biotin martin fib penguin harlequin sequin palanquin ruin bruin win twin dioxin thyroxin toxin yin pinyin muezzin kiln damn goddamn condemn solemn contemn limn column autumn hymn inn jinn

bon gibbon ribbon ebon bonbon carbon hydrocarbon bourbon con bacon beacon deacon archdeacon flacon icon orthicon helicon silicon lexicon falcon soupcon zircon don radon cotyledon myrmidon abandon tendon mastodon pardon guerdon cordon eon melodeon widgeon dudgeon gudgeon bludgeon curmudgeon pigeon dungeon burgeon surgeon sturgeon luncheon puncheon truncheon escutcheon pantheon nucleon chameleon galleon napoleon neon peon hereon thereon whereon chiffon decagon flagon nonagon paragon dragon tarragon tetragon octagon pentagon heptagon wagon hexagon trogon argon jargon gorgon polygon cabochon siphon antiphon colophon marathon telethon python

ion ion suspicion coercion scion accordion contagion legion region religion stanchion fashion refashion cushion pincushion lion battalion dandelion perihelion aphelion ganglion vermilion pavilion scallion medallion stallion rebellion hellion billion million pillion trillion cotillion sextillion zillion bullion scullion mullion thermion anion companion minion dominion pinion opinion amnion onion quaternion union bunion reunion communion nonunion grunion disunion champion scorpion clarion criterion carrion

sion occasion abrasion suasion persuasion dissuasion evasion invasion adhesion cohesion lesion decision indecision precision circumcision incision concision excision elision collision derision misprision vision revision prevision division subdivision envision provision supervision emulsion repulsion impulsion compulsion expulsion avulsion revulsion convulsion scansion mansion expansion ascension condescension reprehension comprehension apprehension in misapprehension declension dimension pension suspension dissension tension pretension extension implosion explosion erosion corrosion submersion immersion aspersion dispersion version aversion subversion reversion diversion inversion conversion perversion torsion incursion excursion passion

ssion compassion cession accession succession recession precession secession concession procession intercession confession profession aggression digression progression transgression depression repression impression compression oppression suppression expression session obsession possession prepossession dispossession scission abscission fission mission submission admission readmission emission remission commission omission permission intermission transmission manumission concussion percussion repercussion discussion fusion effusion diffusion infusion confusion profusion seclusion inclusion conclusion exclusion elusion delusion allusion illusion disillusion collusion prolusion intrusion protrusion contusion

bation-cation

libation probation reprobation approbation disapprobation exacerbation perturbation vacation exsiccation hypothecation deprecation imprecation syllabication eradication abdication dedication indication vindication adjudication syllabification specification edification solidification modification deification qualification vilification jollification amplification exemplification simplification signification indemnification personification unification scarification clarification verification glorification nitrification purification falsification versification diversification classification ossification ratification gratification stratification rectification sanctification fructification quantification identification notification fortification mortification justification mystification revivification publication multiplication implication complication application supplication duplication reduplication explication fornication communication excommunication prevarication fabrication extrication mastication domestication intoxication defalcation suffocation location collocation dislocation translocation vocation avocation revocation equivocation invocation convocation provocation demarcation altercation confiscation coruscation education

dation gradation degradation depredation sedation elucidation validation invalidation consolidation dilapidation trepidation liquidation oxidation emendation commendation recommendation pr inundation foundation accommodation retardation recordation laudation denudation sudation exudation ideation permeation delineation creation recreation procreation

gation propagation variegation legation delegation allegation negation abnegation aggregation congregation obligation fumigation irrigation litigation mitigation castigation investigation instigation navigation promulgation elongation prolongation rogation derogation supererogation prorogation interrogation purgation subjugation conjugation

iation emaciation depreciation appreciation enunciation denunciation renunciation annunciation pronunciation pr association dissociation radiation irradiation mediation repudiation retaliation conciliation reconciliation humiliation foliation spoliation calumniation expiation variation inebriation excoriation appropriation expropriation striation expatiation initiation propitiation vitiation substantiation differentiation negotiation aviation deviation alleviation abbreviation embarkation

lation halation inhalation exhalation ablation oblation elation relation correlation revelation inflation dilation annihilation assimilation compilation ventilation mutilation installation crenellation compellation appellation constellation illation vacillation oscillation distillation collation machicolation violation immolation desolation isolation consolation contemplation legislation translation confabulation tribulation perambulation ejaculation peculation speculation articulation gesticulation calculation miscalculation inoculation circulation osculation adulation undulation modulation coagulation regulation triangulation strangulation ululation emulation simulation dissimulation stimulation formulation accumulation granulation manipulation stipulation copulation population depopulation insulation congratulation expostulation

mation

defamation amalgamation acclamation declamation reclamation proclamation exclamation desquamation cremation sublimation acclimation animation reanimation intimation estimation inflammation summation consummation affirmation confirmation formation reformation malformation information conformation transformation inhumation exhumation

nation

nation profanation explanation emanation alienation concatenation venation stagnation impregnation indignation designation resignation assignation combination vaccination ratiocination fascination hallucination ordination subordination insubordination foreordination imagination origination machination declination inclination disinclination lamination contamination examination dissemination elimination recrimination discrimination culmination abomination domination predomination nomination denomination germination termination determination extermination illumination indoctrination urination assassination procrastination destination predestination ruination divination damnation condemnation conation donation coronation impersonation   intonation   carnation   incarnation   hibernation alternation consternation subornation lunation

| **pation** | anticipation participation emancipation dissipation constipation   palpation   exculpation   extirpation usurpation occupation preoccupation pupation |

| **ration** | ration declaration exhilaration reparation preparation separation   celebration   equilibration   vibration adumbration lucubration desecration consecration |

execration dehydration aeration liberation deliberation reverberation laceration   maceration   ulceration   incarceration   evisceration confederation consideration moderation vociferation exaggeration refrigeration botheration acceleration toleration conglomeration numeration   enumeration   generation   degeneration   regeneration veneration   incineration   remuneration   operation   cooperation exasperation desperation vituperation commiseration iteration obliteration   alliteration   transliteration   alteration   adulteration asseveration   conflagration   integration   disintegration   migration emigration   transmigration   admiration   aspiration   respiration transpiration inspiration perspiration suspiration expiration oration elaboration   corroboration   decoration   adoration   deterioration discoloration exploration commemoration evaporation corporation incorporation   peroration   expectoration   restoration   narration aberration serration susurration penetration perpetration arbitration infiltration concentration registration administration demonstration prostration   illustration   duration   transfiguration   fulguration inauguration   abjuration   adjuration   conjuration   suppuration maturation gyration

| **sation-tation** | pulsation   condensation   compensation |

dispensation sensation conversation cessation causation accusation lactation affectation expectation dictation eructation vegetation interpretation habitation cohabitation citation recitation solicitation resuscitation meditation agitation imitation limitation delimitation exploitation precipitation palpitation irritation hesitation visitation gravitation invitation exaltation occultation auscultation consultation exultation recantation incantation plantation indentation lamentation ornamentation segmentation pigmentation augmentation fomentation fermentation argumentation presentation representation ostentation sustentation confrontation notation annotation potation rotation quotation adaptation acceptation temptation dissertation flirtation exhortation importation transportation exportation station devastation manifestation gestation molestation detestation protestation attestation incrustation refutation confutation salutation mutation commutation transmutation deputation reputation amputation imputation computation disputation

uation-zation

evacuation graduation valuation attenuation extenuation insinuation continuation discontinuation equation menstruation infatuation actuation punctuation situation accentuation excavation lavation aggravation depravation elevation salivation derivation privation deprivation cultivation captivation salvation ovation renovation innovation starvation observation reservation preservation conservation relaxation taxation annexation vexation fixation localization vocalization realization nationalization generalization centralization neutralization equalization visualization mobilization demobilization volatilization fertilization civilization in crystallization formulization systemization legitimization vulcanization organization reorganization disorganization humanization galvanization feminization fraternization polarization

formularization   pulverization   authorization   dramatization
systematization acclimatization

| **action** | action redaction reaction abreaction faction benefaction stupefaction rarefaction putrefaction liquefaction satisfaction dissatisfaction inaction |

compaction counteraction fraction refraction diffraction infraction traction subtraction detraction retraction contraction abstraction distraction attraction extraction transaction exaction

| **ection** | defection affection disaffection infection confection perfection imperfection abjection objection subjection ejection dejection rejection injection projection |

interjection election selection reflection inflection predilection collection recollection connection circumspection inspection introspection erection direction indirection correction resurrection insurrection section vivisection intersection dissection detection protection convection

| **iction-uction** | diction contradiction addiction malediction valediction benediction prediction interdiction jurisdiction fiction dereliction |

affliction infliction friction restriction constriction eviction conviction sanction distinction extinction unction function junction injunction conjunction disjunction compunction decoction infarction auction abduction adduction deduction reduction seduction induction conduction production reproduction underproduction introduction ruction obstruction destruction instruction construction reconstruction misconstruction suction

| **etion-ition** | deletion repletion completion accretion secretion |

concretion discretion indiscretion excretion inhibition prohibition exhibition ambition tradition extradition addition edition expedition sedition rendition condition perdition audition erudition coalition ebullition abolition demolition volition inanition ignition cognition recognition definition monition admonition premonition ammunition punition coition apparition contrition attrition nutrition malnutrition parturition acquisition requisition inquisition disquisition transition position juxtaposition deposition preposition imposition composition decomposition proposition apposition opposition supposition presupposition interposition disposition predisposition indisposition transposition postposition exposition petition repetition competition dentition partition superstition fruition tuition intuition

| **ntion-rtion** | mention detention retention intention contention abstention distention attention inattention |

contravention subvention prevention invention convention reconvention intervention lotion motion emotion demotion commotion locomotion promotion notion potion devotion caption deception reception inception conception misconception perception exception conniption subscription description prescription transcription inscription conscription proscription superscription redemption exemption gumption resumption presumption consumption assumption option adoption sorption absorption eruption interruption irruption corruption disruption desertion insertion assertion exertion overexertion abortion portion proportion disproportion apportion contortion distortion extortion

| **stion-xion** | bastion suggestion digestion indigestion ingestion congestion question exhaustion combustion caution precaution retribution |

contribution distribution consecution prosecution persecution execution locution elocution circumlocution ablution elution dilution pollution solution absolution resolution irresolution dissolution evolution devolution revolution involution convolution diminution substitution destitution restitution institution constitution prostitution oblivion flexion complexion

kon-ron beckon reckon gonfalon encephalon salon talon felon echelon melon watermelon biathlon epsilon upsilon gallon carillon bouillon colon eidolon solon nylon pylon cinnamon daemon demon lemon salmon gammon backgammon mammon persimmon common uncommon summon gnomon sermon ichneumon anon canon phenomenon xenon chignon mignon cannon pennon phonon boon baboon coon raccoon cocoon tycoon buffoon goon lagoon dragoon typhoon loon saloon pantaloon doubloon balloon moon honeymoon noon forenoon afternoon lampoon harpoon spoon teaspoon macaroon picaroon maroon croon quadroon octoroon poltroon soon monsoon bassoon platoon pontoon cartoon festoon spittoon swoon capon weapon crampon tampon pompon tarpon upon hereupon thereupon whereupon coupon baron macron micron omicron squadron tetrahedron octahedron polyhedron caldron cauldron rhododendron heron aileron ephemeron chaperon deuteron saffron iron sadiron gridiron andiron flatiron environ boron moron oxymoron apron negatron matron dynatron patron electron citron positron plastron neutron neuron chevron

son-zon son reason unreason treason season mason freemason diapason grandson godson meson liaison bison malison benison venison unison poison comparison orison prison imprison garrison jettison keelson nelson damson crimson chanson boson stepson arson parson person lesson caisson ton baton megaton automaton phaeton skeleton endoskeleton

94

exoskeleton simpleton piton triton graviton nekton plankton canton wanton badminton fronton wonton photon kiloton proton lepton krypton carton phlogiston piston cotton button unbutton glutton mutton futon mouton crouton sexton gluon won axon claxon klaxon yon rayon crayon halcyon canyon baryon carryon blazon emblazon horizon

arn-urn barn darn earn learn relearn unlearn outlearn yearn tarn warn forewarn yarn concern unconcern discern modern fern northern southern tern lectern lantern intern stern astern eastern northeastern southeastern pastern western northwestern southwestern cistern postern slattern pattern bittern extern quern cavern tavern govern misgovern cairn born stubborn freeborn reborn baseborn highborn wellborn stillborn inborn unborn firstborn suborn newborn lowborn corn acorn unicorn popcorn scorn barleycorn adorn horn shoehorn leghorn bighorn longhorn pronghorn foghorn inkhorn bullhorn greenhorn tinhorn shorn unshorn thorn blackthorn althorn shorthorn hawthorn lovelorn forlorn morn porn torn worn timeworn careworn unworn shopworn sworn forsworn outworn urn burn windburn sunburn heartburn auburn churn inurn adjourn sojourn mourn spurn turn return taciturn downturn upturn overturn outturn

un-wn faun bun dun fun gun handgun begun antigun shogun popgun shotgun outgun blowgun shun nun noun pronoun pun spun homespun run rerun forerun overrun pressrun outrun sun stun dawn predawn fawn lawn pawn spawn brawn drawn redrawn withdrawn overdrawn outdrawn prawn sawn yawn hewn roughhewn strewn bestrewn sewn own down rubdown facedown takedown comedown touchdown pushdown breakdown lockdown markdown turndown rundown sundown letdown meltdown shutdown showdown lowdown slowdown gown nightgown shown blown overblown flyblown clown flown mown renown known unbeknown unknown brown crown uncrown drown frown grown ingrown overgrown outgrown thrown overthrown sown disown town midtown hometown boomtown downtown uptown

14. WORDS ENDING IN LETTER - O

o limbo combo gumbo jumbo hobo lobo turbo bubo guanaco taco tobacco sirocco morocco stucco deco medico calico alnico politico portico flamenco bronco junco rococo loco fiasco fresco alfresco disco ado avocado tornado desperado dorado tostado bravado torpedo redo credo tuxedo libido dildo commando crescendo decrescendo kendo innuendo condo rondo undo dodo overdo hairdo weirdo outdo escudo pseudo judo video rodeo oleo cameo mimeo stereo vireo info ago lumbago archipelago imago virago farrago sago ego superego forego sego indigo amigo impetigo vertigo ginkgo hidalgo fandango mango tango bingo dingo jingo lingo flamingo gringo bongo logo embargo cargo largo ergo undergo forgo outgo macho nacho gazpacho echo reecho rancho honcho poncho psycho mho oho who tallyho

io bio nuncio radio presidio audio studio adagio arpeggio pistachio seraglio intaglio imbroglio punctilio olio folio portfolio polio lothario scenario impresario cheerio oratorio barrio trio curio fellatio patio ratio

jo banjo dojo shako whacko wacko gecko gingko buffalo halo cattalo pueblo tangelo tupelo kilo silo hallo cello violoncello bordello hello armadillo ocotillo bolo piccolo gigolo tremolo polo solo modulo demo memo fortissimo ultimo ammo promo gismo machismo sumo gizmo volcano oregano piano pompano soprano guano keno steno albino bambino chino rhino amino domino palomino merino neutrino casino wino mono kimono inferno porno

oo boo bugaboo taboo bamboo booboo coo skidoo hoodoo

voodoo goo yahoo boohoo shoo ballyhoo cuckoo igloo halloo
waterloo moo shampoo kangaroo buckaroo too cockatoo tattoo woo
zoo kazoo

tempo hippo hypo typo faro taro saguaro macro micro hydro hero
ranchero antihero bolero sombrero torero vaquero zero subzero
nonzero allegro pro repro semipro burro metro retro cilantro intro
maestro bistro chiaroscuro gyro tyro peso proviso also virtuoso
calypso verso torso lasso gesso espresso staccato legato tomato
vibrato moderato potato perfecto recto magneto hereto thereto
whereto veto graffito incognito bonito burrito mosquito alto rialto
contralto canto pimiento lento memento pimento into pinto onto
pronto unto hereunto thereunto whereunto photo esparto quarto
concerto hitherto manifesto presto gusto mulatto ghetto stiletto
palmetto libretto falsetto ditto lotto motto grotto risotto auto duo
continuo bravo octavo centavo salvo servo two kayo arroyo embryo
bozo scherzo matzo palazzo terrazzo mezzo

15. WORDS ENDING IN LETTER - P

ap-ep cap mobcap hubcap madcap redcap icecap kneecap recap whitecap handicap blackcap skullcap uncap nightcap snowcap skycap heap cheap leap overleap neap reap gap stopgap hap chap mishap whap mayhap lap clap thunderclap flap earflap overlap burlap slap backslap dewlap map nap kidnap snap unsnap catnap soap pap rap crap scrap trap satrap rattletrap firetrap mantrap entrap claptrap strap flytrap wrap rewrap enwrap unwrap sap pinesap tap wiretap swap yap zap beep deep cheep sheep jeep keep upkeep barkeep bleep sleep asleep peep creep seep steep weep sweep upsweep schlep julep pep demirep prep step sidestep lockstep instep overstep doorstep misstep footstep yep

ip dip hip chip ship headship friendship hardship stewardship lordship apprenticeship comradeship discipleship reship flagship kingship clerkship generalship steamship guardianship seamanship horsemanship workmanship penmanship citizenship kinship companionship championship relationship unship township scholarship starship warship membership leadership partnership ownership mastership airship ambassadorship authorship censorship professorship dictatorship proprietorship survivorship worship courtship fellowship ladyship whip horsewhip bullwhip skip lip blip clip unclip harelip flip fillip slip cowslip tulip oxlip nip turnip snip parsnip catnip pip rip scrip drip grip handgrip trip strip airstrip outstrip sip gossip tip wingtip quip equip reequip yip zip unzip

lp-mp alp scalp help whelp kelp yelp gulp pulp amp camp decamp encamp scamp damp firedamp champ lamp clamp unclamp headlamp sunlamp ramp cramp tramp tamp stamp vamp revamp swamp hemp temp imp gimp chimp skimp limp blimp pimp crimp scrimp shrimp primp wimp comp chomp clomp pomp romp tromp stomp ump bump dump hump chump thump jump lump clump plump slump mump pump rump frump grump trump sump stump

op-sp

bop bebop cop fop hop chop hedgehop bellhop carhop shop teashop bakeshop grogshop bishop archbishop bookshop workshop pawnshop toyshop lop clop develop overdevelop envelop flop scallop gallop wallop dollop lollop trollop plop slop mop coop hencoop scoop goop hoop whoop loop sloop snoop poop nincompoop droop troop stoop swoop pop lollipop lollypop crop outcrop drop backdrop gumdrop raindrop teardrop airdrop eavesdrop dewdrop snowdrop prop trop strop sop milksop hyssop sysop top atop hardtop treetop tabletop housetop rooftop ragtop blacktop desktop hilltop maintop laptop tiptop overtop stop backstop nonstop unstop doorstop flattop carp endocarp scarp harp sharp tarp warp twerp chirp thorp burp slurp usurp asp gasp hasp clasp unclasp rasp grasp wasp lisp crisp wisp cusp

up-yp

cup teacup hiccup eyecup eggcup buttercup scup speedup buildup holdup standup windup roundup shakeup makeup pileup lineup shapeup ketchup touchup smashup pushup breakup backup crackup checkup pickup stickup lockup mockup walkup linkup hookup lookup markup cleanup pinup sunup grownup coup recoup croup group subgroup regroup soup stoup pup slipup chirrup stirrup syrup sup tossup catsup getup letup setup startup dustup cutup blowup yawp gyp polyp

up-yp

bazaar bar cinnabar sandbar debar sidebar bulbar lumbar unbar lobar isobar disbar crossbar crowbar car handcar sidecar vicar stockcar railcar tramcar motorcar scar flatcar boxcar radar cheddar cedar calendar

16. WORDS ENDING IN LETTER - R

ear

ear bear forebear bugbear overbear forbear dear endear fear gear headgear footgear hear rehear overhear shear mishear blear clear unclear nuclear cochlear smear besmear near linear bilinear rectilinear interlinear pear appear reappear disappear spear rear drear sear tear wear eyewear skiwear neckwear swimwear rainwear underwear swear forswear knitwear footwear outwear playwear year midyear yesteryear

far-sar

far afar insofar gar agar vinegar beggar cigar vulgar hangar cougar sugar char liar familiar unfamiliar peculiar briar friar caviar jar ajar scalar velar burglar similar dissimilar cellar patellar stellar interstellar pillar caterpillar collar dollar medullar alveolar scholar molar premolar polar bipolar dipolar circumpolar solar vacuolar exemplar poplar tabular nebular fibular somnambular lobular globular tubular macular vernacular oracular spectacular molecular secular orbicular acicular perpendicular follicular funicular ventricular auricular particular ocular jocular binocular monocular tubercular circular semicircular noncircular vascular muscular crepuscular corpuscular glandular modular nodular regular irregular angular triangular equiangular quadrangular rectangular singular jugular cellular intracellular copular popular unpopular insular consular capsular titular ovular uvular mar grammar planar coplanar laminar seminar columnar sonar lunar oar boar roar uproar soar par spar feldspar registrar quasar pulsar bursar hussar

tar-zar

tar avatar nectar scimitar sitar guitar altar plantar tartar mortar star lodestar polestar costar daystar attar guar jaguar samovar war prewar antiwar postwar boyar alcazar czar

ber-cer saber gabber rehabber jabber blabber clabber drabber grabber stabber bibber fibber gibber libber bobber jobber clobber slobber robber lubber blubber rubber scrubber grubber fiber caliber briber scriber subscriber transcriber amber camber chamber bedchamber antechamber clamber ember member remember disremember limber climber unlimber timber bomber comber somber umber cumber encumber cucumber dumber lumber plumber slumber number renumber outnumber goober sober barber absorber disturber dauber tuber prefacer lacer placer pacer spacer racer bracer tracer soccer dicer deicer officer artificer nicer choicer ricer juicer ulcer cancer dancer lancer romancer necromancer advancer fencer silencer pincer bouncer denouncer grocer scarcer fiercer mercer forcer enforcer saucer traducer adducer reducer seducer producer

der deader header leader pleader reader spreader loader breechloader broader abrader masquerader grader trader crusader evader invader wader adder ladder bladder gladder madder sadder shedder redder shredder bidder kidder odder dodder fodder plodder prodder udder shudder rudder feeder bleeder speeder breeder seeder wickeder raider abider cider decider eider glider solider slider snider embroider rapider spider stupider rider outrider insider consider reconsider topsider outsider divider provider wider alder balder elder fielder wielder welder milder builder guilder wilder bewilder older bolder colder scolder folder holder landholder beholder officeholder freeholder candleholder shareholder householder upholder molder smolder polder solder unsolder boulder shoulder dander oleander meander gander coriander blander highlander philander colander slander islander salamander demander commander pomander pander expander grander sander stander bystander squander wander ender bender ascender fender defender offender gender engender lender blender slender mender spender suspender expender render surrender sender tender pretender bartender extender vender lavender provender remainder attainder binder bookbinder cinder finder hinder kinder blinder cylinder minder reminder rejoinder grinder tinder winder fonder blonder ponder wonder yonder under launder maunder thunder blunder plunder bounder founder flounder expounder rounder grounder sounder sunder asunder

decoder encoder exploder brooder harder larder boarder hoarder warder herder birder weirder girder order border suborder recorder reorder preorder disorder murder marauder excluder colluder louder prouder ruder cruder intruder extruder lewder shrewder chowder powder gunpowder

eer beer deer killdeer reindeer cheer sheer jeer leer buccaneer veneer mountaineer engineer domineer mutineer pioneer electioneer auctioneer sneer peer compeer career freer seer foreseer overseer sightseer privateer musketeer muleteer volunteer charioteer steer gazetteer queer veer

fer deafer cockchafer loafer safer wafer defer reefer briefer refer prefer gaffer chaffer differ stiffer offer coffer scoffer proffer buffer duffer bluffer snuffer puffer suffer stuffer heifer lifer conifer rifer rotifer aquifer pilfer golfer chamfer infer confer gofer hoofer roofer woofer twofer surfer transfer

ger eager meager uneager overeager packager lager pillager villager imager manager tanager teenager pager forager sager massager stager ravager salvager wager dowager voyager badger cadger hedger ledger abridger codger dodger lodger besieger integer sandbagger dagger nagger bragger dragger stagger swagger bigger digger chigger jigger snigger rigger trigger outrigger fogger defogger pettifogger jogger logger flogger bugger debugger hugger slugger mugger smugger snugger tiger divulger

anger danger endanger hanger changer manger ranger granger arranger stranger challenger passenger messenger avenger scavenger harbinger finger forefinger ginger linger malinger slinger ringer stringer wringer singer stinger winger swinger zinger conger longer monger fishmonger ironmonger sponger stronger hunger plunger lounger younger expunger astrologer booger roger charger larger enlarger merger verger forger burger auger

her her bleacher preacher teacher poacher lecher richer sepulcher rancher drencher trencher quencher clincher pincher launcher stauncher puncher ocher moocher archer searcher marcher scorcher pinscher catcher flycatcher matcher snatcher dispatcher watcher etcher sketcher stretcher ditcher snitcher pitcher switcher botcher butcher blucher voucher higher burgher laugher rougher tougher calligrapher lexicographer geographer stenographer topographer typographer photographer cryptographer cipher decipher encipher gopher philosopher basher dasher flasher masher rasher brasher crasher thrasher washer fresher thresher fisher kingfisher publisher polisher finisher extinguisher ravisher swisher kosher harsher usher gusher blusher plusher pusher rusher crusher bather feather pinfeather heather leather breather weather father grandfather godfather forefather stepfather gather lather blather slather rather ether together altogether whether nether tether dither either neither hither thither whither blither slither wither zither anther panther other bother mother grandmother godmother stepmother smother another smoother soother pother brother stepbrother farther further bier glacier

ker baker beaker bleaker sneaker speaker breaker housebreaker weaker faker shaker maker shoemaker wigmaker matchmaker watchmaker bookmaker mapmaker carmaker dressmaker lawmaker croaker taker partaker undertaker backer hacker whacker hijacker blacker slacker smacker packer cracker firecracker nutcracker tracker sacker stacker attacker checker pecker woodpecker wrecker bicker dicker trafficker thicker whicker kicker clicker flicker slicker mimicker snicker picker sicker ticker sticker quicker wicker cocker shocker locker mocker knocker rocker pucker trucker sucker bloodsucker tucker sleeker meeker seeker biker hiker moniker piker striker trekker talker stalker walker sleepwalker floorwalker banker canker danker hanker blanker flanker spanker ranker franker tanker thinker linker blinker clinker pinker drinker sinker tinker stinker honker bunker debunker hunker clunker drunker choker joker smoker booker cooker hooker looker onlooker snooker poker broker pawnbroker stoker barker darker marker sparker starker shirker corker porker worker coworker lurker asker masker esker whisker brisker frisker husker tusker hawker

ler baler dealer healer realer sealer stealer squealer revealer inhaler whaler dialer signaler paler wholesaler teetotaler staler abler fabler enabler babbler dabbler nibbler scribbler quibbler cobbler gobbler feebler ambler gambler rambler trembler dissembler nimbler fumbler humbler grumbler tumbler nobler warbler chronicler saddler meddler intermeddler peddler fiddler toddler idler handler chandler swindler hurdler dawdler labeler libeler modeler feeler heeler wheeler kneeler peeler chiseler dueler crueler traveler leveler reveler sniveler jeweler baffler shuffler muffler trifler finagler haggler giggler juggler smuggler struggler inveigler angler wrangler bungler bugler bailer hailer jailer mailer frailer trailer detailer retailer reconciler filer defiler profiler miler boiler spoiler despoiler broiler toiler compiler beguiler viler caviler eviler reviler shackler tackler heckler fickler tickler stickler buckler truckler sparkler caller smaller taller smeller impeller propeller speller expeller seller reseller bookseller teller dweller filler chiller killer miller shriller thriller tiller stiller holler roller droller controller stroller extoller frivoller duller fuller cruller condoler choler cooler caroler consoler frivoler stapler ampler sampler simpler grappler tippler suppler coupler twirler curler hurler subtler antler gentler wrestler whistler hostler hustler rustler battler rattler prattler tattler settler whittler littler butler mauler fouler ruler brawler crawler trawler bowler fowler howler prowler dazzler embezzler guzzler puzzler

mer reamer creamer screamer dreamer streamer steamer defamer lamer blamer flamer inflamer roamer framer gossamer tamer redeemer schemer blasphemer dulcimer primer timer embalmer calmer palmer hammer slammer rammer stammer yammer dimmer shimmer skimmer glimmer slimmer grimmer primmer trimmer simmer swimmer bummer glummer mummer drummer strummer summer midsummer comer newcomer homer monomer astronomer misnomer boomer bloomer roomer handsomer isomer customer farmer charmer warmer firmer dormer former reformer informer conformer performer transformer exhumer consumer polymer

ner leaner cleaner meaner planer loaner saner larcener obscener deadener gardener hardener keener screener greener congener freshener wiener darkener sullener opener serener oftener softener whitener fastener listener moistener fattener rottener scrivener campaigner foreigner signer designer cosigner gainer plainer explainer trainer strainer obtainer retainer entertainer vainer diner finer definer refiner shiner whiner liner recliner eyeliner milliner airliner jetliner outliner miner examiner coiner joiner purloiner mariner diviner solemner limner banner scanner planner manner spanner tanner inner dinner beginner thinner skinner spinner sinner winner gunner runner forerunner stunner boner falconer abandoner pardoner goner parishioner pensioner missioner commissioner stationer exhibitioner practitioner petitioner questioner executioner loner almoner commoner schooner lampooner crooner sooner coroner prisoner toner stoner darner earner learner garner southerner sterner corner burner sojourner mourner turner vintner partner copartner tuner fawner owner downer landowner frowner doer evildoer foregoer filmgoer forgoer playgoer wooer

per per caper escaper cheaper reaper shaper diaper japer kidnaper paper notepaper wastepaper wallpaper tarpaper newspaper flypaper scraper draper taper beeper deeper keeper gamekeeper storekeeper housekeeper innkeeper shopkeeper barkeeper doorkeeper sleeper peeper creeper steeper weeper sweeper leper worshiper caliper sniper juniper piper sandpiper bagpiper riper striper viper wiper scalper helper camper scamper damper hamper pamper tramper tamper temper distemper whimper simper romper bumper thumper jumper plumper stumper doper interloper cooper blooper snooper trooper roper proper improper toper capper dapper clapper flapper kidnapper snapper whippersnapper crapper scrapper trapper wrapper sapper swapper pepper stepper dipper chipper shipper worshipper kipper skipper clipper flipper slipper nipper ripper gripper tripper stripper sipper tipper zipper copper hopper chopper shopper grasshopper whopper lopper popper cropper dropper eavesdropper topper stopper upper scupper crupper supper carper sharper usurper jasper vesper whisper crisper prosper pauper duper grouper trouper super hyper

rer barer darer bearer talebearer dearer hearer clearer nearer wearer seafarer wayfarer sharer declarer sparer rarer squarer soberer sincerer sorcerer slanderer panderer wanderer blunderer plunderer murderer sheerer queerer sufferer pilferer swaggerer lingerer gatherer serer caterer slaughterer loiterer falterer adulterer plasterer fosterer chatterer flatterer bitterer mutterer cleverer severer deliverer discoverer fairer repairer direr hirer admirer inspirer acquirer inquirer borer laborer corer scorer adorer explorer poorer sorer restorer favorer referrer stirrer abhorrer demurrer securer procurer obscurer figurer abjurer adjurer conjurer perjurer demurer scourer dourer pourer sourer devourer purer surer measurer treasurer censurer insurer usurer manufacturer lecturer adventurer torturer nurturer

ser baser debaser releaser appeaser greaser teaser chaser purchaser laser maser eraser raiser merchandiser miser riser advertiser bruiser cruiser adviser deviser reviser wiser falser cleanser merganser censer licenser denser condenser dispenser tenser loser closer looser poser composer coarser hoarser parser sparser endorser courser purser gasser amasser passer trespasser harasser crasser lesser dresser redresser hairdresser presser expresser kisser pisser grosser fusser user abuser accuser diffuser nonuser mouser espouser rouser carouser grouser trouser hawser dowser browser geyser

ater debater cater eater beater heater cheater theater amphitheater neater repeater greater anteater sweater hater skater later relater idolater mater oater boater floater rater crater grater prater water seawater rosewater freshwater dishwater breakwater backwater doubter character rejecter specter respecter contradicter indicter stricter sphincter

eter deter fleeter greeter teeter sweeter tweeter budgeter catheter dieter quieter picketer marketer meter diameter hexameter decimeter millimeter perimeter colorimeter centimeter ammeter ohmmeter pedometer odometer udometer dynamometer thermometer seismometer manometer galvanometer chronometer barometer micrometer hygrometer electrometer spectrometer peter trumpeter saltpeter interpreter after hereafter thereafter rafter drafter defter shifter lifter snifter drifter sifter swifter crofter softer yachter straighter fighter prizefighter bullfighter lighter slighter brighter tighter daughter granddaughter stepdaughter laughter slaughter manslaughter

iter gaiter waiter biter arbiter orbiter inciter exciter whiter liter milliliter politer miter niter igniter goiter loiter reconnoiter writer typewriter rewriter titer alter falter halter palter exalter shelter smelter welter swelter filter philter kilter tilter defaulter

nter-rter banter canter decanter chanter enchanter planter granter pleasanter enter center reenter experimenter fomenter carpenter renter presenter dissenter frequenter inter fainter painter quainter hinter splinter

110
Books-India.com - Flipped English Dictionary

minter jointer pointer printer sprinter sinter disinter winter midwinter gaunter haunter saunter bunter hunter chunter blunter counter encounter punter scoter rioter remoter promoter keynoter scooter footer hooter shooter looter rooter tooter voter nonvoter adapter chapter scepter tempter prompter adopter barter darter garter charter smarter tarter starter quarter thwarter deserter inverter flirter comforter shorter exhorter porter reporter importer supporter transporter exporter sorter

ster

aster alabaster caster feaster faster blaster pilaster plaster master ringmaster schoolmaster quartermaster postmaster paymaster boaster coaster roaster toaster raster disaster taster poetaster vaster waster lobster mobster roadster oldster ester fester digester jester jokester molester gamester semester nester pester forester tester sequester southwester dragster gangster songster youngster register blister glister mister banister canister minister administer sinister cloister moister roister chorister barrister sister resister twister huckster pollster bolster holster teamster hamster muenster spinster monster punster foster paternoster booster rooster poster imposter roster tapster hipster tipster quipster buster duster adjuster luster baluster bluster cluster fluster muster ouster thruster shyster oyster

tter-vter

batter scatter fatter hatter chatter shatter latter clatter flatter platter splatter matter smatter patter spatter ratter tatter squatter swatter better fetter unfetter begetter letter newsletter fretter setter wetter bitter embitter fitter hitter jitter skitter litter flitter glitter aglitter splitter slitter emitter remitter transmitter knitter critter fritter sitter titter quitter twitter atwitter otter cotter hotter blotter plotter potter spotter trotter totter utter butter abutter rebutter cutter gutter shutter clutter flutter aflutter splutter mutter putter sputter stutter tauter cuter neuter refuter diluter polluter muter commuter outer accouter shouter flouter pouter router computer pewter presbyter

uer-ver rescuer leaguer vaguer haranguer arguer bluer revenuer lacquer exchequer conquer brusquer truer pursuer issuer aver cadaver beaver cleaver weaver shaver palaver slaver braver graver engraver saver quaver waver ever fever whichever achiever believer unbeliever misbeliever reliever retriever lever clever whomever never whenever whoever whomsoever whosoever whatsoever howsoever wherever forever sever dissever whatever however waiver diver skydiver deceiver receiver giver forgiver lawgiver shiver skiver liver deliver sliver conniver river driver screwdriver upriver arriver contriver striver quiver aquiver reviver salver silver quicksilver solver absolver revolver over cover bedcover recover uncover discover holdover makeover takeover moreover hangover hover pushover walkover lover clover glover allover rollover pullover plover mover remover turnover slipover popover stopover rover drover approver leftover layover carver server observer preserver maneuver louver

wer-zer drawer ewer fewer hewer viewer reviewer interviewer skewer newer brewer sewer bower embower cower dower widower shower lower blower flower deflower co safflower cauliflower bellflower cornflower sunflower mayflower gillyflower glower sallower mellower follower slower mower power willpower empower manpower overpower rower grower thrower narrower borrower tower answer indexer fixer mixer boxer gayer layer bricklayer player slayer payer taxpayer grayer prayer sprayer betrayer soothsayer assayer dyer conveyer shyer flyer slyer coyer foyer employer destroyer dryer fryer spryer wryer buyer lawyer sawyer gazer blazer grazer geezer sneezer freezer oxidizer seizer energizer moralizer atomizer scrutinizer fraternizer temporizer appetizer panzer boozer kibitzer howitzer seltzer analyzer quizzer buzzer

ir   air midair fair affair unfair funfair hair chair armchair horsehair longhair maidenhair mohair lair flair debonair pair repair impair despair corsair stair nadir heir coheir their weir fir kefir whir fakir emir souvenir boudoir choir memoir noir peignoir abattoir devoir reservoir tapir sir grandsir stir astir bestir triumvir elixir

bor-mor   labor belabor tabor neighbor arbor harbor succor decor rancor picador toreador ambassador matador humidor cuspidor corridor candor splendor vendor condor odor malodor ardor meteor for mortgagor obligor rigor vigor clangor abhor anchor anaphor metaphor camphor phosphor author senior seignior junior inferior superior ulterior anterior interior posterior exterior prior warrior excelsior behavior misbehavior savior major squalor valor temblor bachelor counselor sailor tailor councilor pallor chancellor color recolor bicolor tricolor multicolor discolor dolor parlor clamor enamor tremor armor humor rumor tumor

nor-sor   nor demeanor misdemeanor manor tenor signor assignor minor donor honor dishonor governor boor door backdoor indoor trapdoor outdoor floor seafloor moor poor spoor vapor torpor stupor emperor conqueror error terror mirror horror furor juror conjuror incisor visor advisor devisor divisor supervisor censor licensor sensor tensor extensor sponsor cursor precursor successor predecessor processor confessor professor aggressor transgressor assessor possessor

ator   indicator vindicator fornicator defalcator locator educator predator delineator creator procreator propagator alligator investigator instigator navigator derogator interrogator compurgator gladiator radiator mediator expiator appropriator negotiator aviator obviator deviator deflator dilator ventilator oscillator collator violator isolator legislator translator perambulator speculator calculator adulator emulator accumulator insulator decimator animator senator vaccinator originator denominator illuminator procrastinator donator resonator participator vibrator hydrator aerator moderator refrigerator numerator generator operator vituperator adulterator respirator conspirator orator decorator commemorator narrator arbitrator concentrator administrator curator procurator gyrator spectator dictator agitator imitator commentator annotator rotator stator testator valuator equator actuator elevator cultivator renovator innovator conservator debtor

ctor   actor redactor reactor factor malefactor benefactor cofactor enactor tractor detractor retractor contractor extractor exactor defector hector objector ejector injector projector lector elector selector reflector collector inspector rector erector director corrector sector bisector detector protector vector indictor constrictor victor evictor doctor proctor abductor adductor inductor conductor nonconductor instructor

etor-tvr   proprietor secretor traitor elicitor solicitor editor coeditor creditor auditor janitor genitor progenitor monitor heritor inquisitor visitor ovipositor compositor expositor competitor suitor servitor cantor grantor warrantor mentor tormentor inventor motor vasomotor rotor captor raptor acceptor receptor preceptor inceptor sculptor sartor castor pastor ancestor investor resistor impostor bettor abettor contributor prosecutor persecutor executor interlocutor coadjutor dilutor tutor languor liquor endeavor favor disfavor flavor savor survivor fervor flexor mayor conveyor purveyor surveyor razor gnarr err shirr burr purr dinosaur pterosaur centaur bur cocklebur cur occur reoccur recur incur concur farceur grandeur coiffeur chauffeur voyageur monsieur jongleur seigneur friseur danseur poseur masseur connoisseur amateur litterateur raconteur saboteur colporteur hauteur liqueur voyeur fur sulfur augur blur slur demur femur lemur murmur our tambour scour dour troubadour four hour lour velour flour colour amour glamour enamour paramour pour downpour outpour sour tour detour contour devour your jodhpur spur larkspur sequitur zephyr satyr martyr

17. WORDS ENDING IN LETTER - S

as-ps bas fracas pancreas whereas gas bias alias cannabis ibis pubis proboscis caddis aegis haggis his rachis this chrysalis oxalis avoirdupois patois travois lapis debris hubris ephemeris verdigris ambergris iris clitoris basis emphasis elephantiasis oasis stasis metastasis exegesis thesis diathesis metathesis antithesis parenthesis synthesis hypothesis nemesis mimesis genesis agenesis biogenesis parthenogenesis cytogenesis paresis dieresis diaphoresis enuresis phthisis crisis amanuensis narcosis mycosis acidosis apotheosis psychosis metamorphosis meiosis tuberculosis osmosis cyanosis gnosis diagnosis hypnosis fibrosis necrosis sclerosis neurosis ketosis mitosis amitosis kurtosis sepsis asepsis ellipsis synopsis chassis epiphysis dialysis analysis paralysis hydrolysis electrolysis clematis gratis ileitis laryngitis bronchitis mephitis colitis nephritis neuritis bursitis mastitis cystitis mantis stephanotis testis glottis epiglottis cutis unguis marquis pelvis axis praxis parataxis geotaxis ethos thermos cosmos apropos rhinoceros asbestos perhaps biceps triceps forceps oops

ass ass contrabass carcass jackass class subclass declass outclass windlass glass wineglass eyeglass isinglass hourglass spyglass landmass compass encompass overpass surpass trespass bypass harass crass grass ryegrass eelgrass cuirass embarrass disembarrass sass

ess access success nonsuccess recess process abscess excess goddess confess profess burgess chess duchess less

bless jobless headless deedless heedless seedless lidless childless landless endless friendless mindless boundless groundless soundless godless foodless bloodless beardless regardless cordless wordless cloudless tubeless faceless placeless graceless voiceless priceless conscienceless fadeless treeless lifeless ageless edgeless changeless nevertheless guileless shameless blameless nameless timeless homeless spineless boneless toneless tuneless shoeless toeless shapeless hopeless careless tireless wireless cureless measureless baseless ceaseless noiseless defenseless senseless purposeless remorseless useless causeless houseless dateless stateless tasteless valueless clueless sleeveless motiveless loveless nerveless aweless eyeless breezeless leafless selfless roofless meaningless wingless speechless matchless fleshless deathless breathless pathless faithless toothless depthless mirthless worthless ruthless merciless remediless bodiless penniless pitiless trackless feckless reckless luckless thankless workless soulless dreamless seamless foamless aimless rimless bottomless armless harmless formless painless rainless brainless stainless chinless skinless sinless winless companionless passionless expressionless functionless motionless moonless weaponless sonless unless sunless hapless sapless sleepless helpless topless fearless tearless starless warless numberless rudderless cheerless peerless featherless fatherless motherless lusterless flowerless powerless airless hairless odorless colorless furless meatless hatless debtless doubtless tactless objectless ductless fretless shiftless sightless thoughtless profitless hitless limitless spiritless fruitless witless guiltless faultless tenantless scentless relentless pointless dauntless countless bootless rootless spotless artless heartless effortless comfortless restless listless resistless exhaustless gutless lawless flawless dewless viewless sexless keyless joyless mess

ness   ness glibness dumbness numbness franticness badness deadness gladness madness sadness oddness headedness handedness mindedness guardedness ruggedness wretchedness hurriedness nakedness wickedness crookedness redness preparedness sacredness blessedness relatedness indebtedness dejectedness sightedness spiritedness heartedness fixedness staidness sordidness aridness vividness baldness mildness wildness oldness boldness coldness grandness kindness unkindness blindness fondness roundness soundness unsoundness goodness hardness awkwardness inwardness forwardness waywardness weirdness loudness lewdness shrewdness scarceness fierceness wideness nudeness rudeness crudeness freeness safeness savageness strangeness largeness hugeness likeness unlikeness haleness maleness paleness agreeableness reasonableness desirableness deplorableness honorableness favorableness profitableness equitableness suitableness unsuitableness inevitableness feebleness nimbleness humbleness nobleness idleness singleness vileness fickleness wholeness suppleness gentleness lameness sameness tameness supremeness extremeness troublesomeness wholesomeness lonesomeness loathsomeness saneness sereneness fineness feminineness genuineness oneness doneness loneness proneness ripeness bareness rareness entireness soreness pureness sureness baseness conciseness falseness closeness looseness moroseness coarseness hoarseness perverseness profuseness abstruseness delicateness sedateness appropriateness lateness deliberateness completeness incompleteness whiteness politeness impoliteness definiteness indefiniteness contriteness oppositeness remoteness acuteness resoluteness muteness minuteness astuteness vagueness blueness opaqueness obliqueness brusqueness graveness forgiveness persuasiveness evasiveness decisiveness repulsiveness impulsiveness expansiveness defensiveness offensiveness pensiveness expensiveness responsiveness discursiveness impassiveness impressiveness oppressiveness submissiveness effusiveness conclusiveness exclusiveness combativeness talkativeness imaginativeness attractiveness protectiveness vindictiveness definitiveness acquisitiveness inquisitiveness sensitiveness receptiveness descriptiveness sportiveness restiveness exhaustiveness diminutiveness

deafness briefness stiffness gruffness selfness aloofness bigness nothingness willingness unwillingness daringness lovingness youngness smugness snugness richness highness roughness thoroughness toughness rashness freshness childishness oafishness selfishness unselfishness sluggishness foolishness girlishness squeamishness womanishness garishness feverishness pettishness roguishness lavishness peevishness harshness lushness flushness smoothness

iness shabbiness laciness raciness iciness readiness steadiness unsteadiness giddiness ruddiness neediness greediness seediness tidiness untidiness moldiness handiness windiness moodiness hardiness foolhardiness tardiness gaudiness bawdiness leafiness puffiness stuffiness caginess edginess fogginess mugginess springiness stinginess sketchiness touchiness fishiness pithiness healthiness filthiness frothiness worthiness seaworthiness unworthiness trustworthiness stickiness silkiness bulkiness pokiness huskiness deadliness friendliness unfriendliness kindliness godliness ungodliness niggardliness cowardliness steeliness likeliness comeliness homeliness loneliness stateliness liveliness loveliness ugliness oiliness wiliness sickliness chilliness silliness cleanliness manliness womanliness slovenliness holiness orderliness neighborliness surliness sprightliness courtliness beastliness unruliness lowliness dreaminess steaminess griminess filminess clamminess gloominess storminess puniness downiness sleepiness dopiness happiness unhappiness dreariness weariness ordinariness hoariness wariness cheeriness airiness hairiness wiriness peremptoriness paltriness easiness uneasiness flimsiness clumsiness nosiness glossiness fussiness business drowsiness fidgetiness craftiness shiftiness loftiness flightiness mightiness haughtiness naughtiness scantiness daintiness emptiness heartiness dirtiness nastiness mistiness frostiness thirstiness mustiness crustiness trustiness fattiness chattiness pettiness prettiness smuttiness heaviness waviness dewiness sexiness foxiness haziness laziness craziness breeziness coziness ooziness dizziness

knes
bleakness weakness blackness slackness thickness sickness seasickness homesickness quickness meekness dankness blankness rankness frankness darkness briskness

lness
diabolicalness realness exceptionalness naturalness unnaturalness casualness unusualness evilness smallness tallness wellness illness stillness dullness fullness coolness dreadfulness needfulness peacefulness gracefulness resourcefulness vengefulness wakefulness blamefulness hopefulness carefulness usefulness hatefulness gratefulness ungratefulness spitefulness tastefulness wastefulness wrongfulness watchfulness bashfulness wrathfulness faithfulness unfaithfulness healthfulness mirthfulness youthfulness truthfulness untruthfulness mercifulness thankfulness skillfulness willfulness harmfulness painfulness sinfulness scornfulness helpfulness tearfulness cheerfulness powerfulness blissfulness respectfulness forgetfulness fretfulness delightfulness frightfulness thoughtfulness deceitfulness fitfulness fruitfulness artfulness boastfulness restfulness trustfulness awfulness lawfulness playfulness joyfulness foulness

mnes-rness

dimness grimness primness trimness calmness warmness firmness glumness leanness cleanness uncleanness meanness suddenness keenness greenness drunkenness openness barrenness rottenness evenness unevenness plainness vainness thinness commonness wantonness sternness stubbornness lioness baroness patroness cheapness deepness dampness limpness plumpness sharpness dearness clearness nearness harness soberness wilderness slenderness tenderness queerness eagerness meagerness bitterness cleverness governess fairness unfairness dourness sourness

sness

heedlessness boundlessness godlessness lifelessness shamelessness homelessness hopelessness carelessness senselessness uselessness selflessness breathlessness faithlessness worthlessness mercilessness fecklessness recklessness thanklessness sleeplessness helplessness fearlessness powerlessness airlessness tactlessness sightlessness thoughtlessness guiltlessness artlessness restlessness listlessness lawlessness grossness hideousness outrageousness erroneousness righteousness unrighteousness courteousness graciousness vivaciousness officiousness maliciousness deliciousness suspiciousness capriciousness viciousness consciousness unconsciousness tediousness fastidiousness odiousness religiousness punctiliousness abstemiousness copiousness seriousness penuriousness luxuriousness seditiousness fictitiousness licentiousness obsequiousness obviousness deviousness lasciviousness zealousness callousness ridiculousness scrupulousness monotonousness pompousness ponderousness boisterousness vigorousness timorousness adventurousness covetousness solicitousness conspicuousness deciduousness contiguousness sumptuousness voluptuousness nervousness joyousness

tness-vness | neatness   greatness   fatness   flatness
compactness   abstractness   exactness
inexactness   directness   correctness   incorrectness   strictness
distinctness indistinctness sweetness quietness wetness daftness
deftness swiftness softness straightness lightness rightness brightness
uprightness   fitness   unfitness   adroitness   witness   pleasantness
unpleasantness faintness bluntness hotness aptness promptness
abruptness corruptness smartness tartness stalwartness alertness
inertness   pertness   expertness   shortness   curtness   fastness
steadfastness vastness earnestness moistness justness tautness
rawness   fewness   newness   lowness   shallowness   mellowness
yellowness hollowness slowness narrowness laxness gayness
grayness shyness slyness coyness dryness spryness busyness

oess-uss | loess cress watercress dress address headdress
redress   undress   laundress   sundress   sorceress
murderess peeress adulteress egress regress aggress
digress tigress ingress congress progress transgress heiress prioress
press depress repress empress impress compress oppress suppress
letterpress express tress actress benefactress directress waitress
enchantress huntress temptress fortress stress distress mistress
schoolmistress seamstress mattress buttress obsess reassess repossess
prepossess prophetess poetess giantess countess hostess guess
outguess prowess gneiss kiss bliss remiss dismiss emboss joss loss
floss gloss cross across uncross crisscross dross gross engross
albatross toss gauss degauss cuss concuss fuss schuss sourpuss truss

bus-nus | bus syllabus rebus minibus omnibus nimbus
rhombus thrombus microbus autobus airbus

succubus incubus abacus umbilicus focus defocus refocus hocus locus crocus circus hibiscus discus meniscus caucus mucus modus exodus caduceus nucleus coleus gluteus sarcophagus esophagus magus asparagus dingus fungus bogus bronchus typhus thus acanthus radius genius jus ruckus talus nautilus callus phallus bacillus bolus embolus nucleolus alveolus plus nonplus surplus calculus oculus modulus stimulus cumulus tumulus annulus stylus mandamus shamus thalamus ignoramus hippopotamus isthmus animus strabismus litmus humus thymus anus manus tetanus subgenus minus terminus sinus alumnus onus bonus tonus

bous-hous gibbous bulbous viscous raucous mucous tremendous stupendous horrendous hazardous sebaceous herbaceous farinaceous saponaceous drupaceous cretaceous siliceous hideous outrageous courageous advantageous disadvantageous gorgeous miscellaneous extemporaneous subterraneous extraneous simultaneous instantaneous spontaneous subcutaneous homogeneous heterogeneous igneous ligneous erroneous calcareous nacreous vitreous gaseous osseous nauseous righteous piteous plenteous bounteous courteous discourteous beauteous duteous aqueous fungous analogous homologous amorphous

ious amphibious dubious efficacious inefficacious mendacious audacious sagacious fallacious contumacious tenacious pugnacious pertinacious capacious rapacious spacious veracious gracious ungracious voracious loquacious vivacious specious precious judicious injudicious officious malicious delicious pernicious auspicious suspicious unsuspicious avaricious capricious meretricious vicious precocious ferocious atrocious conscious subconscious unselfconscious unconscious luscious tedious perfidious insidious fastidious invidious compendious odious melodious unmelodious commodious incommodious studious contagious sacrilegious egregious prodigious religious irreligious litigious contumelious bilious supercilious punctilious rebellious abstemious ingenious calumnious symphonious euphonious felonious ceremonious unceremonious acrimonious parsimonious harmonious inharmonious unharmonious impecunious pious impious copious carious precarious vicarious nefarious gregarious hilarious uproarious various opprobrious lugubrious salubrious insalubrious imperious serious deleterious mysterious delirious laborious glorious inglorious vainglorious censorious victorious meritorious notorious uxorious industrious illustrious curious overcurious furious injurious penurious spurious usurious luxurious ostentatious unostentatious vexatious factious fractious infectious facetious ambitious expeditious seditious flagitious propitious unpropitious nutritious fictitious repetitious supposititious adventitious surreptitious superstitious licentious conscientious pretentious unpretentious sententious contentious captious bumptious scrumptious cautious incautious obsequious obvious devious previous lascivious oblivious envious pervious impervious anxious overanxious noxious obnoxious

| **lous** | scandalous jealous zealous anomalous troublous libelous marvelous perilous scurrilous callous villous frivolous parlous fabulous nebulous bibulous miraculous ridiculous |

meticulous credulous incredulous sedulous pendulous scrofulous emulous tremulous cumulous populous scrupulous unscrupulous querulous garrulous patulous edentulous

| **mou** | famous infamous bigamous exogamous ramous blasphemous pusillanimous magnanimous unanimous |

venomous   autonomous   dichotomous   enormous   posthumous
anonymous synonymous eponymous

nous | diaphanous   membranous   indigenous   endogenous
homogenous   nitrogenous   exogenous   venous   ravenous
villainous mountainous libidinous multitudinous heinous
mucilaginous cartilaginous ferruginous ominous conterminous
leguminous luminous voluminous numinous bituminous resinous
gelatinous glutinous mutinous ruinous vinous tyrannous stannous
poisonous monotonous gluttonous cavernous androgynous pulpous
pompous

rous | barbarous   viviparous   oviparous   nectarous   scabrous
glabrous   fibrous   cumbrous   ludicrous   polyandrous
wondrous   hydrous   anhydrous   tuberous   ulcerous
cancerous slanderous ponderous thunderous murderous calciferous
vociferous   viniferous   somniferous   carboniferous   coniferous
odoriferous auriferous lactiferous dangerous treacherous lecherous
numerous innumerous generous onerous obstreperous viperous
prosperous serous adulterous dipterous boisterous preposterous
dexterous cadaverous desirous chivalrous decorous indecorous
rancorous odorous rigorous vigorous clangorous phosphorous
valorous dolorous amorous clamorous timorous humorous sonorous
porous vaporous traitorous languorous herbivorous omnivorous
carnivorous insectivorous leprous cuprous ferrous idolatrous nitrous
disastrous   estrous   monstrous   lustrous   ambidextrous   aurous
sulphurous venturous adventurous rapturous

tous-vous | acetous covetous felicitous solicitous calamitous
precipitous   necessitous   circuitous   iniquitous
gratuitous   fortuitous   filamentous   momentous

portentous riotous vacuous transpicuous conspicuous inconspicuous perspicuous nocuous innocuous promiscuous deciduous assiduous arduous ambiguous unambiguous contiguous exiguous superfluous ingenuous disingenuous strenuous tenuous sinuous continuous congruous incongruous sensuous fatuous anfractuous unctuous impetuous spirituous tumultuous contemptuous sumptuous presumptuous voluptuous virtuous tortuous tempestuous flexuous mischievous grievous nervous rendezvous joyous

| pus-ws | pus campus grampus rumpus opus octopus corpus lupus platypus uterus virus walrus chorus phosphorus pylorus cirrus susurrus citrus estrus thesaurus papyrus |

rhesus nisus census consensus tarsus metatarsus versus excursus narcissus missus colossus hiatus flatus afflatus apparatus status cactus ictus fetus quietus impetus coitus emeritus detritus lotus eucalyptus arbutus nevus plexus nexus gallows

18. WORDS ENDING IN LETTER - T

bat-lat

bat dingbat brickbat combat wombat acrobat cat bobcat wildcat polecat hellcat tomcat scat requiescat ducat copycat pussycat concordat eat beat deadbeat offbeat drumbeat downbeat upbeat browbeat feat defeat heat cheat escheat reheat preheat superheat overheat wheat buckwheat bleat cleat pleat meat crabmeat forcemeat sweetmeat nutmeat neat peat repeat thereat whereat overeat great threat treat retreat maltreat entreat mistreat seat reseat backseat unseat teat caveat sweat fat nonfat nougat hat chat chitchat hardhat shat that what somewhat fiat lariat commissariat proletariat blat flat mudflat plat splat slat

mat-wat

mat bathmat diplomat format reformat doormat gnat oat boat iceboat lifeboat fireboat longboat tugboat keelboat sailboat steamboat gunboat airboat flatboat showboat rowboat towboat ferryboat coat redcoat bluecoat petticoat tailcoat raincoat turncoat topcoat undercoat overcoat greatcoat waistcoat goat scapegoat shoat bloat float afloat gloat moat throat cutthroat stoat pat spat rat carat baccarat karat brat theocrat democrat aristocrat autocrat drat frat muskrat sprat ziggurat sat tat habitat appestat rheostat hemostat thermostat aerostat cryostat kumquat squat vat cravat swat twat

bt-ct

debt doubt redoubt misdoubt act redact react fact artifact enact reenact pact impact compact cataract bract interact counteract overact refract diffract infract tract subtract detract retract contract protract abstract distract attract extract misact transact tact intact contact exact inexact playact pandect defect prefect affect disaffect effect infect disinfect perfect imperfect abject object subject eject deject reject inject project interject dialect elect reelect select deselect deflect reflect inflect neglect intellect collect recollect connect disconnect aspect respect disrespect circumspect inspect prospect retrospect suspect expect erect direct redirect indirect misdirect correct incorrect sect bisect trisect vivisect transect insect intersect dissect detect architect protect contradict addict edict maledict benedict predict indict interdict verdict relict derelict afflict inflict conflict depict strict restrict district constrict evict convict mulct sacrosanct succinct precinct distinct indistinct instinct extinct defunct adjunct conjunct decoct concoct infarct duct viaduct abduct adduct deduct aqueduct oviduct induct conduct misconduct product eruct usufruct obstruct destruct instruct construct reconstruct

et

bet abet alphabet rabbet gibbet gobbet sherbet facet videlicet scilicet dulcet lancet avocet faucet cadet bidet beet feet clubfeet forefeet flatfeet sheet parakeet lorikeet skeet fleet sleet meet unmeet helpmeet discreet indiscreet greet street sweet bittersweet tweet buffet get gadget fidget midget widget budget beget nugget target retarget forget cachet sachet ricochet crochet hatchet ratchet crotchet nymphet prophet freshet epithet whet diet quiet unquiet disquiet soviet jet inkjet ramjet twinjet turbojet propjet jacket straitjacket placket packet racket bracket thicket picket cricket pricket ticket wicket docket locket pocket pickpocket rocket sprocket socket bucket blanket trinket junket market basket workbasket casket gasket brisket musket let chalet valet tablet giblet driblet goblet doublet sublet circlet bracelet lancelet omelet corselet platelet wavelet eyelet leaflet eaglet piglet ringlet pamphlet filet toilet anklet booklet ballet mallet pallet wallet pellet billet fillet skillet millet bullet gullet mullet pullet streamlet hamlet gimlet armlet inlet moonlet runlet flageolet violet caplet chaplet triplet droplet couplet scarlet starlet varlet underlet coverlet islet gantlet frontlet gauntlet rootlet tartlet cutlet outlet epaulet amulet rivulet owlet met helmet grommet plummet unmet comet gourmet kismet calumet net planet genet tenet magnet electromagnet dragnet signet cygnet fishnet cabinet spinet clarinet bassinet martinet gillnet gannet jennet rennet linnet bonnet sonnet falconet baronet coronet bayonet carnet garnet cabernet hairnet cornet hornet brunet poet pet parapet limpet crumpet trumpet strumpet lappet tappet whippet snippet tippet moppet puppet carpet ret cabaret caret claret minaret secret beret spinneret floweret fret egret regret floret interpret garret ferret turret set subset headset handset mindset beset typeset reset preset offset backset thickset quickset inset onset moonset unset sunset closet marmoset upset overset corset asset basset cosset gusset russet outset heavyset octet quintet motet septet quartet stet sestet sextet duet minuet racquet piquet sobriquet banquet coquet croquet parquet bouquet cruet suet vet brevet civet rivet privet trivet velvet covet duvet wet rewet yet

ft-ht

aft abaft daft haft shaft camshaft raft craft witchcraft handicraft aircraft draft redraft updraft overdraft graft engraft waft deft heft theft left cleft bereft weft gift shift makeshift lift forklift shoplift uplift airlift rift drift adrift snowdrift shrift thrift spendthrift sift resift swift delft oft loft aloft hayloft soft tuft yacht borscht straight bight eight height sleight freight weight hundredweight middleweight overweight lightweight fight dogfight bullfight gunfight outfight light alight blight headlight delight candlelight limelight firelight flight searchlight torchlight twilight fanlight penlight moonlight sunlight plight lamplight starlight slight gaslight daylight skylight might night midnight knight tonight overnight fortnight right aright bright fright affright birthright forthright alright downright upright outright wheelwright playwright copyright sight foresight eyesight insight oversight tight uptight airtight caught uncaught onslaught naught draught fraught distraught taught untaught ought bought fought thought bethought forethought aforethought afterthought brought drought wrought inwrought unwrought overwrought sought besought unsought borsht

it bait redbait parfait gait plait trait portrait strait distrait wait await outwait bit megabit gigabit habit inhabit cohabit rabbit hobbit tidbit debit rarebit inhibit prohibit exhibit backbit ambit gambit obit kilobit orbit frostbit cubit tacit deficit licit elicit illicit solicit implicit explicit edit reedit credit accredit discredit copyedit bandit pundit audit plaudit albeit howbeit deceit conceit counterfeit forfeit surfeit fit befit benefit refit comfit discomfit unfit profit retrofit misfit outfit legit digit hit chit shit bullshit whit kit skit weskit lit alit floodlit flit twilit moonlit unlit sunlit split starlit slit submit resubmit admit readmit emit demit reemit remit limit delimit commit recommit summit omit vomit hermit permit intermit transmit manumit nit knit snit unit whodunit exploit adroit introit pit fleapit sandpit decrepit pipit cockpit pulpit armpit spit cesspit inherit merit demerit preterit grit spirit dispirit inspirit culprit sprit esprit bowsprit writ sit housesit visit revisit transit posit deposit exposit tit petit tomtit circuit biscuit conduit quit acquit bruit recruit fruit breadfruit grapefruit suit swimsuit jumpsuit pursuit pantsuit lawsuit snowsuit playsuit bodysuit intuit davit affidavit wit pewit dimwit twit nitwit outwit exit fixit zit

lt alt cobalt dealt misdealt halt asphalt malt salt basalt desalt gestalt exalt belt sunbelt felt unfelt heartfelt melt smelt snowmelt knelt pelt spelt welt dwelt gilt hilt jilt kilt lilt milt spoilt spilt silt tilt stilt built rebuilt guilt quilt wilt bolt deadbolt eyebolt kingbolt ringbolt unbolt thunderbolt colt dolt holt jolt molt volt revolt kilovolt fault default assault vault cult occult difficult adult tumult penult catapult result insult consult exult dreamt

ant ant cant vacant decant recant secant cosecant mendicant indicant significant insignificant applicant lubricant vesicant toxicant intoxicant scant descant pedant confidant oxidant commandant ascendant descendant defendant pendant dependant attendant fondant abundant superabundant redundant verdant accordant discordant mordant pageant sergeant leant meant unmeant recreant procreant miscreant bouffant infant termagant extravagant elegant inelegant fumigant litigant arrogant chant enchant penchant trenchant disenchant merchant elephant triumphant sycophant re insouciant radiant irradiant defiant giant valiant reliant brilliant pliant compliant suppliant variant luxuriant deviant sealant nonchalant inhalant exhalant assailant sibilant jubilant vigilant gallant topgallant repellant appellant coolant plant replant eggplant implant supplant transplant slant aslant ambulant undulant stimulant petulant adamant claimant dormant informant tenant lieutenant revenant covenant stagnant regnant pregnant indignant malignant benignant poignant repugnant complainant dominant predominant determinant ruminant remnant pennant sonant resonant consonant inconsonant assonant dissonant pant participant rampant flippant occupant rant vibrant quadrant hydrant protuberant exuberant preponderant refrigerant tolerant intolerant itinerant operant adulterant perseverant grant flagrant fragrant vagrant migrant emigrant spirant aspirant colorant cormorant ignorant sonorant arrant warrant errant aberrant currant entrant ministrant remonstrant restaurant courant tyrant pheasant pleasant unpleasant peasant complaisant obeisant versant conversant passant incessant croissant puissant recusant combatant blatant reactant disinfectant expectant octant reluctant habitant inhabitant exorbitant militant precipitant irritant hesitant visitant annuitant resultant exultant accountant important unimportant contestant protestant distant equidistant assistant instant constant inconstant adjutant mutant disputant extant sextant piquant truant pursuant savant relevant irrelevant servant observant unobservant maidservant manservant adjuvant want relaxant abeyant buoyant clairvoyant cognizant

ent bent lambent decumbent recumbent incumbent unbent absorbent cent adjacent complacent accent decent indecent recent beneficent magnificent munificent reticent demulcent docent innocent percent scent ascent nascent descent iridescent incandescent turgescent quiescent coalescent convalescent adolescent obsolescent evanescent crescent excrescent phosphorescent florescent fluorescent putrescent deliquescent effervescent reminiscent lucent translucent dent decadent decedent precedent antecedent accident occident incident coincident diffident confident overconfident trident strident resident president evident provident improvident transcendent resplendent pendent dependent independent superintendent indent despondent respondent correspondent rodent ardent mordent impudent prudent imprudent student gent agent subagent reagent regent indigent negligent diligent intelligent unintelligent exigent indulgent fulgent refulgent effulgent plangent tangent stringent astringent contingent pungent cogent argent margent emergent detergent divergent convergent urgent ambient stupefacient deficient efficient inefficient sufficient insufficient proficient ancient nescient prescient omniscient gradient obedient disobedient expedient ingredient salient client ebullient lenient convenient inconvenient sapient recipient incipient percipient impercipient orient reorient nutrient prurient esurient transient patient impatient sentient dissentient quotient subservient lent exhalent talent tetravalent prevalent bivalent divalent trivalent equivalent covalent relent silent pestilent excellent repellent redolent indolent violent somnolent insolent malevolent benevolent turbulent flocculent succulent feculent esculent luculent truculent fraudulent opulent corpulent virulent purulent flatulent

| **ament** | predicament lineament ligament parliament lament filament armament firmament ornament tournament sacrament temperament testament entombment oddment commandment amendment bombardment |

| **ement** | cement defacement placement replacement displacement advancement commencement renouncement announcement pronouncement enforcement reinforcement divorcement seducement inducement agreement disagreement engagement management mismanagement disparagement encouragement discouragement acknowledgement derangement arrangement disarrangement estrangement infringement enlargement rapprochement vehement rabblement ennoblement clement inclement element entanglement reconcilement defilement revilement implement complement supplement battlement settlement unsettlement embezzlement tenement refinement confinement postponement atonement escapement elopement decrement excrement retirement acquirement requirement procurement disfigurement allurement measurement basement abasement debasement casement easement advertisement chastisement advisement reimbursement disbursement amusement abatement statement restatement overstatement misstatement incitement excitement denouement bereavement pavement achievement involvement movement improvement amazement aggrandizement |

| **gment-ymant** | fragment acknowledgment abridgment lodgment judgment segment figment |

pigment augment encroachment detachment attachment enrichment parchment bewitchment refreshment blandishment establishment embellishment accomplishment banishment admonishment astonishment garnishment punishment impoverishment nourishment relinquishment ravishment raiment pediment impediment sediment condiment embodiment rudiment regiment aliment habiliment compliment accompaniment liniment orpiment experiment merriment detriment nutriment sentiment presentiment embankment concealment ailment entailment curtailment despoilment devilment installment fulfillment comment enlightenment arraignment alignment consignment assignment ordainment detainment entertainment attainment abandonment disillusionment apportionment environment imprisonment discernment government adornment adjournment foment moment entrapment shipment equipment encampment development endearment garment undergarment dismemberment bewilderment wonderment ferment deferment preferment interment averment impairment torment amassment harassment embarrassment assessment treatment enactment indictment besetment revetment commitment enchantment disenchantment resentment presentment contentment discontentment ointment appointment disappointment allotment apartment department compartment deportment assortment vestment investment adjustment abutment hutment document tegument integument argument emolument monument instrument endowment payment repayment enjoyment employment

ent anent immanent permanent eminent preeminent imminent prominent continent incontinent pertinent impertinent abstinent deponent component opponent exponent pent repent serpent spent unspent misspent outspent rent parent apparent transparent deferent referent afferent efferent different indifferent vicegerent belligerent adherent inherent coherent incoherent reverent irreverent deterrent torrent current recurrent concurrent undercurrent quitrent sent absent resent present represent misrepresent omnipresent consent unsent assent dissent tent latent patent competent incompetent appetent penitent renitent intent content discontent potent omnipotent impotent portent insistent consistent inconsistent persistent existent nonexistent intermittent extent unguent fluent affluent effluent influent frequent infrequent sequent subsequent consequent inconsequent delinquent eloquent grandiloquent magniloquent constituent vent advent event nonevent prevent solvent insolvent circumvent invent reinvent convent fervent went forewent underwent forwent

int
faint plaint complaint paint repaint restraint constraint saint taint attaint quaint acquaint dint feint hint lint flint gunflint glint splint mint spearmint varmint peppermint joint conjoint disjoint anoint point midpoint standpoint endpoint pinpoint embonpoint gunpoint appoint disappoint counterpoint viewpoint pint print reprint preprint offprint imprint sprint misprint footprint tint aquatint stint squint

ont
font piedmont front seafront forefront affront confront wont learnt unlearnt burnt aunt daunt gaunt haunt jaunt flaunt taunt vaunt bunt exeunt hunt headhunt manhunt shunt outhunt foxhunt blunt count account recount discount miscount viscount fount mount amount paramount remount surmount dismount punt runt brunt grunt stunt jabot sabot abbot robot turbot cot picot haricot apricot tricot ascot mascot wainscot dot got fagot begot faggot maggot bigot gigot spigot ingot argot escargot ergot forgot hot shot bloodshot birdshot eyeshot buckshot gunshot snapshot upshot earshot undershot overshot hotshot potshot idiot riot

chariot antiriot patriot compatriot cheviot jot lot zealot blot inkblot clot feedlot sandlot bibelot ocelot helot polyglot pilot copilot allot ballot shallot maillot plot subplot complot marplot grassplot harlot slot mot bergamot marmot not pinot knot unknot slipknot topknot cannot snot whatnot

oot

boot reboot jackboot coot scoot foot afoot webfoot clubfoot barefoot forefoot flatfoot hotfoot crowfoot hoot shoot offshoot overshoot outshoot loot moot snoot root bloodroot cheroot taproot uproot arrowroot soot toot

pot-ypt

pot teapot depot coffeepot repot firepot jackpot crackpot stockpot inkpot stinkpot spot despot eyespot sunspot fusspot rot tarot carrot parrot trot dogtrot foxtrot tommyrot sot tot aliquot divot pivot

apt

apt adapt readapt leapt periapt inapt unapt rapt enrapt accept reaccept precept incept concept percept intercept except adept kept slept overslept inept crept transept wept unwept swept windswept upswept receipt script subscript nondescript transcript conscript postscript manuscript sculpt preempt unkempt tempt contempt attempt exempt prompt opt adopt readopt excerpt abrupt erupt bankrupt interrupt irrupt corrupt incorrupt disrupt crypt decrypt encrypt

art-urt

art cart teacart handcart dogcart pushcart dumpcart oxcart dart heart sweetheart fart braggart hart chart mart smart outsmart part apart subpart depart forepart rampart impart counterpart tart start redstart restart upstart quart wart thwart athwart stalwart swart filbert concert disconcert alert inert pert malapert expert inexpert desert insert reinsert assert reassert dessert dissert avert obvert subvert advert revert divert culvert invert convert overt covert introvert controvert pervert exert overexert dirt girt begirt engirt shirt nightshirt skirt flirt quirt squirt ort abort escort fort effort comfort discomfort cohort short exhort snort port seaport deport homeport report heliport import comport rapport support carport airport purport sport disport transport passport jetport export sort resort presort consort assort tort retort contort distort extort cavort fleawort soapwort curt yogurt hurt unhurt blurt court spurt

ast
bombast cast broadcast telecast typecast recast forecast downcast overcast miscast newscast outcast east beast feast northeast southeast least breast abreast redbreast yeast fast steadfast bedfast breakfast aghast scholiast enthusiast last blast ballast leucoplast outlast mast foremast mizzenmast mainmast topmast gymnast dynast boast coast seacoast roast toast past repast pederast contrast vast midst amidst

est
best lest lamest tamest calmest dimmest slimmest grimmest primmest trimmest glummest handsomest warmest firmest nest leanest cleanest meanest sanest keenest greenest serenest oftenest plainest vainest finest tannest thinnest honest dishonest commonest soonest earnest sternest pest cheapest anapest deepest steepest ripest tempest plumpest flippest sharpest crispest rest barest dearest clearest nearest sparest rarest squarest crest headrest soberest sincerest slenderest sheerest queerest merest serest interest bitterest cleverest severest fairest direst backrest armrest unrest forest deforest reforest poorest sorest arrest footrest securest demurest dourest sourest purest surest wrest basest wisest falsest densest tensest closest loosest coarsest hoarsest sparsest crassest grossest test neatest greatest latest strictest detest fleetest sweetest quietest retest pretest deftest swiftest softest straightest lightest

slightest brightest tightest whitest politest pleasantest faintest quaintest contest gauntest bluntest remotest protest promptest smartest tartest shortest fastest vastest moistest attest fattest flattest wettest fittest hottest posttest tautest cutest mutest minutest guest vaguest bluest quest bequest request inquest conquest truest vest bravest gravest divest invest reinvest harvest west rawest fewest newest northwest southwest lowest shallowest sallowest slowest narrowest gayest grayest shyest slyest coyest spryest wryest zest angst amongst

ist ultraist waist cubist pharmacist racist ethicist publicist empiricist lyricist physicist romanticist exorcist fascist sadist faddist orthopedist rhapsodist nudist deist heist theist atheist monotheist canoeist fist pacifist gist strategist druggist genealogist mineralogist archaeologist ideologist geologist psychologist ornithologist bacteriologist physiologist philologist entomologist penologist phrenologist meteorologist herpetologist eulogist theurgist schist sophist whist list cabalist vocalist idealist realist legalist specialist socialist materialist finalist annalist nationalist rationalist journalist moralist pluralist muralist naturalist fatalist capitalist individualist sensualist spiritualist conceptualist loyalist royalist cyclist panelist duelist novelist pugilist nihilist cellist enlist reenlist violist fabulist somnambulist wrist lyrist subsist desist resist insist consist persist assist twist against

ost cost accost host ghost lost most headmost midmost endmost hindmost middlemost foremost headforemost almost inmost easternmost topmost rearmost nethermost furthermost innermost uppermost uttermost outermost utmost outmost glasnost boost roost post bedpost milepost gatepost goalpost impost compost signpost lamppost rudderpost outpost frost defrost hoarfrost prost provost first thirst athirst worst burst sunburst outburst exhaust bust combust robust locust dust stardust sawdust gust disgust august just adjust readjust unjust lust must oust joust roust rust crust piecrust encrust incrust thrust antirust trust entrust distrust mistrust cyst nematocyst amethyst analyst catalyst tryst watt megawatt kilowatt mitt boycott

ut-xt | butt mutt putt haut ablaut umlaut aquanaut aeronaut juggernaut kraut sauerkraut taut but abut debut rebut halibut cut woodcut precut uncut linocut undercut uppercut haircut crosscut shortcut gut catgut hut shut jut glut slut gamut smut nut peanut thumbnut pignut beechnut doughnut walnut hazelnut coconut donut butternut chestnut out bout about gadabout roundabout hereabout thereabout runabout rubout scout readout foldout holdout handout standout hideout shakeout takeout stakeout flameout timeout wipeout closeout whiteout gout ragout hangout dugout mahout pitchout throughout shout washout without breakout blackout checkout lockout knockout walkout cookout lookout workout lout clout flout bailout fallout sellout rollout pullout rainout spinout burnout turnout snout brownout pout dropout spout waterspout rout grout sprout trout tout setout printout shootout stout cutout shutout putout devout blowout layout carryout tryout buyout put kaput input output rut brut strut newt next text subtext pretext context hypertext twixt betwixt

19. WORDS ENDING IN LETTER - U

u landau eau beau flambeau bandeau tableau chapeau bureau trousseau bateau chateau plateau portmanteau nouveau fabliau luau adieu lieu milieu purlieu snafu tofu fichu juju haiku seppuku flu ormolu lulu menu submenu parvenu gnu inconnu marabou caribou thou kinkajou bijou you bayou ecru guru zaibatsu shiatsu jujitsu impromptu

20. WORDS ENDING IN LETTER - W

aw caw macaw jackdaw guffaw gewgaw haw chaw heehaw trishaw kickshaw rickshaw cumshaw thaw jaw lockjaw law claw flaw windflaw scofflaw slaw coleslaw outlaw bylaw maw gnaw mackinaw paw papaw forepaw southpaw raw craw draw redraw withdraw overdraw outdraw straw bedstraw saw handsaw seesaw foresaw jigsaw hacksaw chainsaw whipsaw ripsaw oversaw taw squaw yaw

ew dew bedew mildew honeydew few curfew hew chew eschew roughhew phew nephew grandnephew cashew whew view review preview interview overview purview skew askew blew clew flew curlew slew mew new anew renew sinew knew foreknew pew spew brew crew aircrew screw jackscrew corkscrew unscrew drew redrew withdrew overdrew outdrew grew overgrew outgrew shrew threw overthrew strew bestrew sew stew yew

ow bow longbow elbow rainbow crossbow oxbow cow scow meadow shadow foreshadow overshadow widow endow reendow window meow how chow chowchow somehow show sideshow reshow peepshow anyhow low bungalow blow below furbelow flow mudflow inflow overflow airflow outflow glow aglow afterglow allow callow fallow hallow shallow mallow sallow disallow tallow wallow swallow bellow fellow playfellow mellow yellow billow pillow willow follow hollow plow snowplow slow mow haymow now know foreknow minnow winnow snow row brow eyebrow highbrow lowbrow crow scarecrow cockcrow escrow windrow hedgerow grow overgrow outgrow throw overthrow cornrow prow arrow barrow handbarrow wheelbarrow harrow marrow narrow sparrow yarrow borrow morrow tomorrow sorrow burrow furrow sow tow undertow stow bestow kowtow vow avow disavow wow bowwow powwow yow

21. WORDS ENDING IN LETTER - X

ax broadax addax poleax fax pickax lax relax flax smilax parallax max climax anticlimax coax hoax anthrax borax thorax hyrax sax tax pretax syntax overtax surtax wax earwax beeswax ibex spandex index codex hex telex flex reflex pollex triplex simplex complex perplex duplex annex apex rex murex sex unisex unsex latex vertex cortex vortex vex convex radix appendix fix prefix affix reaffix suffix crucifix infix unfix transfix postfix helix bollix prolix mix admix remix premix commix intermix nix phoenix pix cicatrix aviatrix matrix executrix six cervix phalanx sphinx jinx minx quincunx lynx pharynx larynx

ox box breadbox feedbox bandbox sandbox icebox saucebox jukebox firebox snuffbox matchbox workbox mailbox pillbox toolbox soapbox gearbox chatterbox sweatbox hatbox saltbox postbox outbox paradox orthodox unorthodox fox outfox lox phlox lummox flummox equinox pox smallpox cowpox sox beaux flambeaux bandeaux tableaux chapeaux bateaux chateaux portmanteaux faux fabliaux adieux flux reflux afflux efflux influx conflux bijoux roux crux tux coccyx calyx onyx

22. WORDS ENDING IN LETTER - Y

bay-ray
bay sickbay decay day workaday faraday midday someday washday birthday holiday weekday workday noonday today yesterday doomsday mayday payday heyday everyday gay nosegay antigay hay shay sashay jay deejay popinjay okay lay clay belay delay relay flay allay inlay play wordplay replay foreplay gunplay downplay underplay overplay airplay splay display misplay outplay parlay underlay interlay overlay slay mislay outlay waylay may dismay nay pay repay prepay underpay overpay spay ray bray chambray dray fray defray affray gray stingray foray moray hooray pray spray array disarray hurray tray betray ashtray portray stray astray

say-way
say daresay soothsay gainsay unsay hearsay assay bioassay essay stay mainstay overstay outstay quay way away foldaway hideaway takeaway areaway seaway giveaway rollaway runaway caraway faraway getaway castaway cutaway stowaway layaway flyaway subway headway roadway speedway midway floodway raceway tideway leeway freeway passageway bikeway someway causeway gateway driveway halfway gangway archway hatchway highway pathway taxiway walkway folkway parkway railway hallway spillway crawlway tramway runway underway waterway airway fairway stairway doorway motorway sway straightway beltway footway partway thruway byway alleyway skyway flyway anyway entryway

by
baby crybaby wallaby lullaby cabby scabby gabby shabby flabby crabby grabby tabby cobwebby bobby hobby lobby knobby snobby cubby hubby chubby clubby scrubby grubby shrubby

tubby stubby standby hereby thereby whereby rugby booby nearby derby passerby ruby flyby

cy abbacy celibacy efficacy inefficacy delicacy indelicacy intricacy advocacy legacy profligacy lacy prelacy fallacy supremacy primacy legitimacy intimacy diplomacy pharmacy contumacy obstinacy lunacy papacy episcopacy racy democracy aristocracy confederacy degeneracy literacy piracy conspiracy magistracy accuracy inaccuracy obduracy testacy adequacy inadequacy privacy fleecy prophecy secrecy icy policy spicy juicy normalcy vacancy mendicancy ascendancy redundancy mordancy fancy infancy extravagancy chancy sycophancy valiancy brilliancy pliancy deviancy adamancy necromancy dormancy tenancy lieutenancy stagnancy pregnancy malignancy poignancy repugnancy discrepancy rampancy occupancy vibrancy vagrancy blatancy expectancy precipitancy hesitancy exultancy constancy inconstancy piquancy truancy conservancy buoyancy lambency complacency decency indecency translucency cadency presidency dependency tendency despondency ardency agency regency exigency tangency astringency contingency pungency cogency emergency urgency deficiency efficiency inefficiency sufficiency insufficiency expediency saliency leniency incipiency percipiency excellency clemency inclemency permanency eminency transparency currency latency competency potency impotency consistency inconsistency fluency frequency infrequency constituency solvency fervency bouncy idiocy mercy bankruptcy saucy

dy beady heady ready already unready steady unsteady shady lady malady landlady milady toady caddy daddy paddy eddy teddy biddy giddy kiddy middy shoddy toddy buddy muddy ruddy needy speedy reedy greedy seedy weedy tweedy tragedy raggedy remedy comedy perfidy subsidy tidy untidy unwieldy moldy bandy candy dandy organdy handy unhandy randy brandy sandy trendy windy burgundy body homebody somebody antibody embody nobody anybody everybody busybody melody psalmody threnody hymnody monody goody bloody moody broody woody parody prosody rhapsody custody hardy foolhardy lardy jeopardy tardy nerdy wordy sturdy gaudy cloudy study restudy understudy bawdy dowdy pandowdy howdy rowdy

ey abbey obey disobey lacey spacey dicey pricey fey cagey bogey boogey hey they whey key lackey dickey hickey hockey jockey latchkey donkey monkey turnkey flunkey hokey pokey malarkey turkey whiskey passkey medley bailey smiley riley alley galley tomalley valley trolley volley pulley barley charley parley burley paisley parsley motley limey homey kidney whiney piney hackney cockney chimney spinney honey baloney money gooney blarney attorney gurney journey tourney jitney chutney gooey hooey phooey dopey palfrey prey lamprey osprey surrey trey malmsey mosey nosey goosey jersey odyssey curtsey chantey maguey gluey cliquey peavey convey covey purvey survey clayey

fy leafy defy beefy stupefy rarefy putrefy liquefy daffy taffy iffy jiffy spiffy huffy chuffy fluffy puffy scruffy stuffy unstuffy syllabify pacify specify calcify decalcify dulcify crucify edify acidify rigidify solidify humidify dandify codify modify deify reify qualify vilify jellify mollify nullify amplify simplify ramify mummify magnify dignify signify minify indemnify unify reunify typify scarify clarify rarify verify glorify terrify horrify petrify nitrify vitrify gentrify purify gasify falsify emulsify intensify versify diversify classify ossify beatify ratify gratify stratify rectify sanctify fructify citify stultify quantify identify notify certify fortify mortify testify justify mystify prettify beautify vivify revivify detoxify comfy goofy scurfy satisfy

gy stagy edgy podgy stodgy sludgy smudgy pudgy elegy strategy baggy shaggy craggy scraggy saggy leggy piggy twiggy boggy doggy foggy smoggy groggy soggy buggy muggy prodigy effigy bulgy slangy mangy rangy tangy dingy clingy springy stringy stingy swingy spongy dungy grungy bogy fogy pedagogy demagogy logy genealogy analogy mineralogy trilogy antilogy pharmacology ecology toxicology oncology mycology ideology geology theology neology phraseology psychology morphology pathology anthology mythology biology sociology bacteriology physiology etiology philology gemology epistemology homology entomology etymology zymology menology penology phrenology technology criminology sinology demonology chronology zoology apology anthropology topology typology necrology serology virology horology petrology astrology urology eschatology hematology herpetology ontology paleontology otology histology cytology sexology doxology eulogy stogy lethargy clergy allergy energy synergy orgy porgy metallurgy zymurgy dramaturgy liturgy

hy achy headachy peachy preachy screechy squelchy paunchy raunchy punchy crunchy anarchy monarchy hierarchy starchy autarchy catchy patchy scratchy sketchy stretchy tetchy itchy bitchy pitchy twitchy botchy blotchy splotchy duchy slouchy grouchy touchy dinghy doughy telegraphy calligraphy lexicography geography orthography biography autobiography radiography bibliography stenography iconography topography typography chirography chromatography photography cryptography trophy atrophy philosophy shy ashy flashy splashy trashy squashy washy fleshy fishy squishy marshy bushy cushy gushy plushy slushy mushy pushy brushy thy breathy apathy telepathy antipathy empathy sympathy osteopathy lengthy smithy pithy healthy unhealthy stealthy wealthy filthy timothy toothy frothy earthy swarthy worthy seaworthy praiseworthy noteworthy unworthy trustworthy untrustworthy mouthy why

ky leaky sneaky peaky creaky freaky streaky squeaky shaky flaky snaky croaky quaky tacky wacky icky colicky garlicky gimmicky panicky finicky picky tricky sticky cocky blocky rocky stocky ducky lucky unlucky plucky mucky yucky cheeky spiky balky chalky talky milky silky bulky sulky hanky lanky cranky swanky inky dinky kinky slinky pinky stinky funky chunky junky clunky flunky spunky smoky hooky kooky spooky poky autarky jerky perky quirky corky murky sky pesky whisky risky frisky bosky dusky husky fluky gawky

aly-bly scaly mealy bialy anomaly ably indescribably probably imperturbably implacably inexplicably amicably despicably inextricably irrevocably readably formidably unavoidably commendably laudably peaceably noticeably agreeably disagreeably interchangeably permeably loveably moveably affably ineffably indefatigably laughably sociably unsociably remediably justifiably reliably amiably deniably undeniably variably invariably insatiably pitiably viably enviably unspeakably unmistakably remarkably unassailably irreconcilably uncontrollably inconsolably inestimably conformably presumably inalienably amenably tenably abominably interminably damnably fashionably unexceptionably unquestionably reasonably unreasonably seasonably unseasonably capably palpably impalpably culpably bearably unbearably reparably irreparably inseparably incomparably drably considerably preferably insufferably tolerably intolerably innumerably miserably unalterably unutterably irrecoverably unanswerably admirably adorably deplorably honorably dishonorably favorably unfavorably inexorably impenetrably demonstrably curably durably measurably immeasurably commensurably indispensably passably usably inexcusably ratably intractably respectably indubitably creditably profitably unprofitably inimitably indomitably hospitably charitably uncharitably veritably irritably equitably suitably inevitably unaccountably notably quotably unacceptably comfortably uncomfortably portably detestably incontestably unstably irrefutably mutably reputably indisputably inscrutably arguably valuably equably unbelievably irretrievably inconceivably lovably movably immovably provably taxably sizably pebbly wobbly bubbly feebly trebly invincibly forcibly irreducibly credibly incredibly audibly inaudibly legibly illegibly eligibly intelligibly unintelligibly incorrigibly tangibly indelibly glibly fallibly infallibly gullibly terribly horribly feasibly risibly visibly divisibly invisibly sensibly insensibly ostensibly reversibly irrepressibly inexpressibly admissibly permissibly possibly impossibly plausibly perceptibly imperceptibly irresistibly inexhaustibly flexibly inflexibly brambly assembly nimbly dumbly humbly numbly crumbly nobly ignobly superbly volubly doubly publicly franticly

dly badly deadly gladly madly broadly sadly oddly cuddly shamefacedly forcedly decidedly underhandedly confoundedly guardedly unguardedly jaggedly raggedly doggedly ruggedly wretchedly variedly hurriedly nakedly wickedly crookedly markedly designedly resignedly unrestrainedly learnedly unconcernedly sacredly tiredly assuredly advisedly unadvisedly composedly supposedly cursedly professedly confusedly amusedly heatedly repeatedly elatedly agitatedly undoubtedly abstractedly distractedly affectedly dejectedly disconnectedly unexpectedly delightedly excitedly conceitedly spiritedly contentedly discontentedly disjointedly pointedly wontedly unwontedly undauntedly bigotedly devotedly uninterruptedly wholeheartedly halfheartedly lightheartedly distortedly interestedly disinterestedly disgustedly admittedly deservedly undeservedly unreservedly avowedly fixedly dazedly idly staidly rabidly morbidly turbidly acidly placidly viscidly lucidly candidly splendidly sordidly rigidly frigidly turgidly validly solidly stolidly timidly rapidly vapidly torpidly stupidly acridly floridly horridly torridly putridly luridly fetidly languidly fluidly avidly lividly vividly fervidly baldly mildly wildly boldly coldly worldly unworldly blandly grandly friendly unfriendly kindly unkindly blindly spindly secondly fondly profoundly roundly soundly godly ungodly goodly niggardly hardly dastardly awkwardly inwardly cowardly untowardly upwardly forwardly southwestwardly outwardly waywardly weirdly thirdly lordly absurdly loudly proudly lewdly shrewdly

ely nicely princely scarcely fiercely snidely widely rudely crudely freely steely safely wifely sagely savagely strangely largely hugely lithely blithely likely unlikely palely facilely docilely agilely futilely vilely solely gamely lamely namely tamely supremely extremely sublimely timely untimely comely uncomely homely handsomely troublesomely wholesomely wearisomely contumely urbanely humanely inanely sanely insanely obscenely serenely finely femininely supinely clandestinely genuinely divinely lonely opportunely inopportunely shapely unshapely

rely

rely barely sparely rarely squarely sincerely insincerely merely austerely severely direly entirely sorely securely insecurely obscurely demurely purely impurely surely leisurely maturely prematurely immaturely

sely

basely precisely concisely wisely unwisely falsely densely immensely tensely intensely closely loosely purposely morosely coarsely hoarsely sparsely tersely aversely adversely inversely conversely perversely transversely diffusely profusely obtusely

tely

delicately indelicately intricately sedately immediately appropriately inappropriately lately disconsolately articulately inarticulately legitimately ultimately intimately proximately approximately inordinately indeterminately obstinately innately passionately compassionately dispassionately affectionately proportionately alternately ornately fortunately unfortunately importunately separately deliberately considerately inconsiderately moderately immoderately temperately desperately irately elaborately accurately inaccurately precipitately stately adequately inadequately privately effetely completely eruditely whitely politely impolitely finitely definitely indefinitely infinitely tritely contritely exquisitely appositely oppositely sveltely remotely chastely unchastely cutely acutely absolutely resolutely mutely minutely astutely

uely-vely

vaguely opaquely obliquely uniquely picturesquely grotesquely brusquely bravely gravely suavely naively coercively lively persuasively evasively decisively derisively repulsively impulsively convulsively defensively offensively apprehensively pensively expensively intensively extensively responsively explosively discursively massively passively impassively successively excessively aggressively progressively repressively impressively oppressively expressively submissively permissively abusively effusively inclusively conclusively exclusively obtrusively unobtrusively intrusively negatively interrogatively appreciatively relatively speculatively affirmatively natively imaginatively alternatively comparatively imperatively vituperatively figuratively meditatively authoritatively argumentatively tentatively actively attractively effectively subjectively reflectively collectively respectively prospectively retrospectively vindictively restrictively distinctively instinctively seductively inductively productively unproductively destructively definitively inquisitively sensitively positively competitively intuitively substantively attentively plaintively descriptively presumptively furtively festively attributively reflexively lovely unlovely

fly
fly deafly gadfly chiefly briefly firefly horsefly housefly stiffly gruffly shoofly aloofly barfly deerfly butterfly mayfly

gly
scraggly straggly giggly squiggly gangly absorbingly disturbingly menacingly enticingly entrancingly convincingly unconvincingly piercingly pleadingly forbiddingly exceedingly commandingly condescendingly correspondingly astoundingly accordingly engagingly disparagingly encouragingly discouragingly grudgingly obligingly stingingly longingly unflinchingly searchingly touchingly laughingly dashingly refreshingly astonishingly unblushingly soothingly kingly painstakingly rollickingly mockingly strikingly unthinkingly jokingly provokingly appealingly ramblingly tremblingly feelingly smilingly sparklingly gallingly appallingly thrillingly willingly unwillingly

consolingly startlingly beamingly seemingly swimmingly becomingly unbecomingly charmingly alarmingly threateningly entertainingly whiningly winningly cunningly questioningly yearningly warningly fawningly gaspingly

ringly | daringly glaringly sparingly unsparingly wonderingly leeringly staggeringly lingeringly witheringly flickeringly falteringly unflatteringly waveringly perseveringly overpoweringly despairingly admiringly enquiringly inquiringly boringly adoringly imploringly unerringly alluringly reassuringly

singly-ugly | singly unceasingly pleasingly increasingly surprisingly imposingly surpassingly pressingly depressingly amusingly tingly deprecatingly excruciatingly humiliatingly ingratiatingly undeviatingly exhilaratingly penetratingly hesitatingly unhesitatingly insinuatingly detractingly affectingly unsuspectingly fleetingly slightingly bitingly excitingly invitingly haltingly meltingly revoltingly insultingly exultingly enchantingly dotingly temptingly sportingly everlastingly unresistingly disgustingly trustingly fittingly wittingly unwittingly unbelievingly lovingly movingly reprovingly approvingly disapprovingly flowingly knowingly unknowingly taxingly vexingly mortifyingly satisfyingly pryingly tryingly pityingly amazingly agonizingly patronizingly strongly wrongly ugly smugly snugly

hly | richly archly churchly highly roughly thoroughly toughly rashly brashly fleshly freshly childishly modishly elfishly selfishly unselfishly sluggishly rakishly devilishly foolishly girlishly mulishly owlishly stylishly sheepishly impishly snappishly foppishly garishly feverishly pettishly roguishly lavishly slavishly peevishly boyishly harshly lushly deathly fifthly eighthly tenthly seventhly ninthly monthly smoothly earthly unearthly fourthly sixthly

| **ily** | daily prickly sickly quickly sleekly meekly weekly biweekly dankly lankly blankly rankly frankly pinkly wrinkly darkly sparkly starkly briskly |

| **ally** | ally tribally globally verbally prosaically syllabically radically medically methodically periodically spasmodically specifically terrifically scientifically |

magically tragically logically genealogically illogically geologically psychologically physiologically etymologically lethargically liturgically hierarchically graphically telegraphically geographically typographically philosophically diabolically symbolically dynamically academically chemically rhythmically inimically comically anatomically cosmically organically mechanically technically clinically tyrannically laconically sardonically chronically ironically electronically platonically microscopically typically spherically atmospherically clerically numerically hysterically satirically allegorically metaphorically rhetorically historically theatrically electrically symmetrically eccentrically lyrically whimsically intrinsically classically musically physically metaphysically

emphatically dramatically mathematically systematically enigmatically asthmatically grammatically automatically ecstatically didactically practically syntactically apoplectically apologetically energetically prophetically pathetically sympathetically hypothetically esthetically genetically poetically theoretically dietetically politically critically uncritically hypocritically romantically frantically idiotically patriotically hypnotically antiseptically elliptically optically cryptically vertically bombastically sarcastically monastically fantastically majestically euphemistically optimistically aphoristically artistically linguistically caustically nautically paradoxically quizzically focally locally reciprocally vocally unequivocally rascally fiscally dally tidally modally feudally ideally lineally really ethereally legally illegally regally prodigally frugally lethally proverbially facially racially specially especially judicially officially unofficially artificially superficially financially provincially socially commercially medially remedially cordially filially genially congenially menially venially ceremonially serially materially dictatorially pictorially industrially mercurially substantially confidentially prudentially tangentially deferentially reverentially essentially potentially consequentially partially impartially colloquially jovially axially formally informally normally abnormally dismally anally banally phenomenally venally signally medicinally longitudinally finally originally criminally nominally pronominally spinally diagonally occasionally provisionally professionally nationally rationally irrationally sensationally conditionally unconditionally intentionally unintentionally conventionally exceptionally proportionally personally impersonally tonally atonally carnally infernally paternally fraternally eternally internally externally vernally faunally communally principally rally liberally generally laterally collaterally literally severally spirally virally orally florally morally amorally centrally ventrally dextrally aurally rurally naturally unnaturally supernaturally preternaturally gutturally sally nasally universally dorsally causally tally fatally rectally congenitally vitally accidentally incidentally mentally fundamentally elementally experimentally detrimentally sentimentally horizontally totally mortally distally brutally dually gradually individually manually continually annually equally unequally squally casually visually sensually usually unusually actually ineffectually intellectually punctually perpetually habitually ritually spiritually eventually virtually mutually sexually loyally royally

| **elly** | belly potbelly sowbelly genteelly jelly smelly tinselly cruelly gravelly levelly frailly dilly filly hilly chilly frilly shrilly silly stilly tranquilly evilly civilly uncivilly dolly |

folly golly holly wholly jolly loblolly molly coolly woolly drolly

| **ully** | bully dully fully dreadfully heedfully peacefully gracefully gleefully balefully dolefully shamefully woefully hopefully carefully irefully remorsefully usefully hatefully |

gratefully ungratefully spitefully ruefully wrongfully reproachfully watchfully bashfully wrathfully faithfully unfaithfully healthfully mirthfully truthfully untruthfully mercifully unmercifully pitifully plentifully bountifully beautifully dutifully thankfully skillfully unskillfully willfully manfully disdainfully painfully sinfully scornfully mournfully helpfully fearfully tearfully wonderfully cheerfully masterfully powerfully successfully unsuccessfully distressfully blissfully doubtfully tactfully respectfully disrespectfully fretfully regretfully delightfully rightfully frightfully thoughtfully deceitfully fitfully resentfully uneventfully artfully boastfully restfully wistfully trustfully distrustfully mistrustfully awfully lawfully unlawfully sorrowfully playfully joyfully gully foully sully

| **mly** | seemly unseemly dimly slimly grimly primly trimly calmly randomly warmly firmly uniformly glumly cleanly meanly manly gentlemanly ungentlemanly unmanly |

womanly unwomanly humanly inhumanly wanly suddenly maidenly

woodenly keenly queenly mistakenly brokenly unbrokenly sullenly openly barrenly rottenly heavenly cravenly evenly unevenly slovenly brazenly frozenly benignly ungainly plainly mainly certainly uncertainly vainly thinly solemnly only curmudgeonly commonly uncommonly matronly sonly wantonly modernly sternly slatternly stubbornly forlornly holy melancholy unholy wooly monopoly

ply cheaply haply deeply steeply reply triply multiply amply damply imply limply pimply simply comply panoply apply reapply misapply supply sharply crisply early dearly clearly nearly linearly pearly yearly biyearly beggarly vulgarly familiarly peculiarly similarly scholarly perpendicularly particularly jocularly circularly regularly irregularly singularly popularly gnarly lubberly somberly soberly elderly tenderly orderly disorderly queerly eagerly meagerly overeagerly gingerly fatherly grandfatherly motherly grandmotherly brotherly northerly southerly soldierly formerly mannerly unmannerly properly improperly dapperly miserly quarterly easterly masterly westerly southwesterly sinisterly sisterly latterly bitterly utterly cleverly overly fairly unfairly girly whirly neighborly poorly burly curly knurly dourly hourly sourly surly

sly measly grisly crassly heedlessly needlessly endlessly gracelessly voicelessly lifelessly shamelessly blamelessly hopelessly carelessly ceaselessly noiselessly defenselessly senselessly uselessly tastelessly breathlessly faithlessly ruthlessly mercilessly pitilessly recklessly aimlessly harmlessly helplessly fearlessly tearlessly cheerlessly peerlessly tactlessly sightlessly thoughtlessly fruitlessly faultlessly relentlessly dauntlessly spotlessly artlessly restlessly listlessly expressly crossly grossly thusly

ously

raucously tremendously hideously outrageously courageously advantageously gorgeously simultaneously instantaneously spontaneously erroneously righteously piteously courteously discourteously dubiously efficaciously audaciously sagaciously tenaciously graciously ungraciously voraciously loquaciously vivaciously speciously judiciously injudiciously officiously maliciously deliciously auspiciously inauspiciously suspiciously avariciously capriciously meretriciously viciously ferociously consciously subconsciously unconsciously tediously insidiously fastidiously melodiously commodiously studiously contagiously egregiously prodigiously religiously litigiously superciliously ingeniously ignominiously feloniously ceremoniously unceremoniously parsimoniously harmoniously piously copiously vicariously uproariously variously imperiously seriously mysteriously deliriously laboriously gloriously notoriously industriously illustriously curiously furiously injuriously luxuriously

ostentatiously facetiously expeditiously fictitiously adventitiously surreptitiously superstitiously licentiously conscientiously sententiously cautiously incautiously obsequiously obviously deviously previously lasciviously enviously anxiously jealously zealously marvelously perilously callously frivolously nebulously miraculously ridiculously meticulously incredulously sedulously tremulously scrupulously querulously famously blasphemously magnanimously unanimously enormously posthumously synonymously ominously voluminously mutinously tyrannously monotonously cavernously pompously barbarously ludicrously wondrously ponderously vociferously dangerously treacherously lecherously numerously generously prosperously boisterously dexterously decorously indecorously rancorously rigorously vigorously valorously dolorously amorously timorously humorously

Books-India.com - Flipped English Dictionary

sonorously porously vaporously disastrously monstrously ambidextrously rapturously covetously felicitously solicitously calamitously precipitously circuitously gratuitously fortuitously conspicuously inconspicuously perspicuously innocuously promiscuously assiduously arduously contiguously superfluously ingenuously strenuously sinuously continuously discontinuously fatuously unctuously impetuously tumultuously contemptuously sumptuously presumptuously virtuously tempestuously mischievously grievously nervously joyously

tly featly neatly greatly flatly subtly compactly abstractly exactly perfectly imperfectly abjectly circumspectly erectly directly indirectly correctly incorrectly strictly succinctly distinctly indistinctly fleetly discreetly sweetly quietly secretly wetly daftly deftly swiftly softly lightly slightly nightly knightly rightly brightly sprightly uprightly unsightly tightly tacitly licitly implicitly explicitly fitly adroitly vacantly significantly insignificantly scantly abundantly discordantly mordantly extravagantly elegantly inelegantly arrogantly triumphantly radiantly defiantly valiantly brilliantly luxuriantly nonchalantly vigilantly gallantly petulantly stagnantly indignantly malignantly resonantly flippantly tolerantly ignorantly pleasantly unpleasantly incessantly expectantly reluctantly distantly instantly constantly complacently decently indecently recently magnificently innocently reminiscently diffidently confidently overconfidently evidently resplendently independently despondently ardently impudently prudently imprudently gently negligently diligently intelligently indulgently pungently cogently urgently sufficiently insufficiently anciently obediently saliently leniently conveniently inconveniently incipiently transiently patiently impatiently silently excellently indolently violently somnolently insolently benevolently turbulently fraudulently virulently vehemently permanently eminently preeminently incontinently pertinently impertinently apparently transparently differently indifferently belligerently coherently incoherently reverently irreverently currently absently presently latently patently competently penitently intently potently impotently inadvertently insistently consistently persistently intermittently fluently frequently infrequently subsequently consequently eloquently fervently faintly saintly quaintly jointly conjointly gauntly bluntly

hotly aptly raptly adeptly ineptly promptly abruptly corruptly smartly partly tartly alertly inertly pertly expertly overtly covertly shortly portly curtly courtly beastly steadfastly ghastly lastly vastly modestly manifestly priestly honestly dishonestly earnestly thistly moistly bristly gristly costly ghostly mostly firstly robustly justly unjustly tautly stoutly devoutly duly unduly unruly truly untruly brawly crawly newly lowly hollowly slowly narrowly laxly shyly slyly coyly dryly spryly wryly drizzly grizzly

my creamy dreamy seamy steamy infamy gamy bigamy endogamy monogamy misogamy exogamy polygamy foamy loamy academy alchemy blasphemy enemy pigmy pygmy limy slimy rimy grimy balmy filmy whammy clammy mammy shimmy jimmy swimmy mommy scummy dummy gummy chummy slummy mummy rummy crummy tummy yummy sodomy physiognomy antinomy economy agronomy astronomy autonomy taxonomy gloomy roomy bosomy anatomy lobotomy craniotomy army barmy smarmy squirmy stormy wormy rheumy fumy plumy synonymy metonymy

ny any tiffany mahogany epiphany miscellany many company accompany litany botany zany larceny deny spleeny teeny progeny villainy rainy brainy grainy shiny sunshiny whiny hominy ignominy spiny briny tiny satiny destiny mutiny scrutiny calumny canny uncanny fanny nanny cranny granny tyranny jenny penny halfpenny sixpenny finny hinny shinny whinny skinny ninny tinny bonny sonny bunny funny unfunny gunny runny sunny bony ebony balcony chalcedony peony agony cosmogony phony symphony euphony polyphony felony colony hegemony lemony ceremony alimony palimony acrimony matrimony patrimony simony parsimony antimony testimony harmony loony moony pony barony crony irony monotony stony cottony gluttony ferny corny horny thorny puny brawny scrawny tawny downy monogyny misogyny

oy boy pageboy homeboy highboy doughboy bellboy schoolboy tomboy carboy paperboy choirboy busboy newsboy batboy cowboy lowboy plowboy playboy copyboy coy decoy ahoy joy killjoy enjoy cloy alloy ploy deploy employ reemploy annoy viceroy troy destroy corduroy soy toy buoy envoy convoy soapy therapy hydrotherapy satrapy sleepy creepy weepy stripy gossipy enthalpy pulpy swampy gimpy skimpy scrimpy wimpy bumpy dumpy jumpy lumpy frumpy grumpy stumpy copy recopy miscopy bioscopy microscopy spectroscopy jalopy canopy goopy loopy snoopy droopy ropy philanthropy misanthropy entropy isotropy happy unhappy nappy snappy pappy crappy scrappy sappy peppy preppy dippy whippy lippy nippy snippy drippy zippy choppy floppy sloppy poppy soppy guppy puppy harpy spy raspy espy crispy wispy occupy reoccupy soupy syrupy

ry peccary apothecary scary dromedary lapidary quandary legendary secondary boundary bleary smeary dreary teary weary vagary vinegary beggary sugary chary beneficiary diary intermediary incendiary stipendiary plagiary auxiliary pecuniary apiary topiary friary penitentiary plenipotentiary tertiary bestiary aviary breviary salary tutelary burglary capillary maxillary corollary epistolary exemplary vocabulary constabulary formulary cartulary rosemary primary palmary mammary summary customary infirmary nary canary granary mercenary plenary binary ordinary extraordinary imaginary disciplinary culinary seminary preliminary luminary veterinary urinary sanguinary visionary reversionary missionary exclusionary stationary reactionary insurrectionary dictionary functionary discretionary precautionary evolutionary revolutionary pulmonary coronary ternary quaternary unary sublunary hoary library supernumerary itinerary vulnerary funerary literary honorary temporary contemporary arbitrary contrary dispensary rosary adversary anniversary bursary necessary unnecessary emissary commissary glossary sectary dietary proprietary planetary monetary secretary undersecretary hereditary military solitary sanitary dignitary unitary depositary pituitary sedentary parliamentary testamentary elementary complementary supplementary fragmentary rudimentary alimentary complimentary uncomplimentary commentary momentary documentary voluntary involuntary notary rotary votary tributary salutary residuary antiquary ossuary statuary actuary sanctuary obituary mortuary estuary vary salivary ovary wary unwary cry decry mimicry descry outcry dry semidry ribaldry heraldry husbandry polyandry laundry foundry sundry wizardry tawdry

| ery | jobbery slobbery snobbery robbery blubbery rubbery shrubbery bribery tracery chancery grocery sorcery doddery shuddery embroidery spidery bindery prudery powdery |

cheery leery puffery midwifery imagery savagery drudgery buggery snuggery gingery forgery surgery treachery lechery archery hatchery witchery butchery debauchery periphery fishery feathery leathery lathery slithery smothery soldiery fiery colliery briery furriery hosiery bakery fakery quackery cookery rookery celery jugglery gallery raillery artillery distillery drollery scullery cajolery foolery tomfoolery cutlery creamery emery flummery mummery summery perfumery deanery scenery greenery venery finery refinery machinery millinery joinery winery cannery tannery gunnery nunnery stationery confectionery buffoonery poltroonery fernery ornery turnery japery napery papery drapery trumpery popery peppery slippery frippery coppery foppery whispery dupery lamasery misery nursery eatery watery cemetery psaltery adultery dysentery effrontery artery mastery monastery upholstery blustery mystery battery clattery flattery jittery glittery lottery pottery tottery buttery fluttery presbytery roguery query very slavery antislavery knavery bravery every thievery shivery livery delivery quivery silvery recovery discovery brewery showery lowery flowery fry refry belfry panfry angry hungry

iry airy dairy nondairy fairy hairy miry expiry enquiry inquiry wiry cavalry chivalry rivalry hostelry revelry jewelry devilry henry citizenry deaconry archdeaconry falconry felonry weaponry masonry freemasonry

ory chicory dory theory gory allegory category priory hickory glory pillory memory armory vapory derisory advisory provisory supervisory compulsory sensory cursory accessory promissory elusory delusory illusory approbatory deprecatory imprecatory judicatory classificatory predatory mandatory commendatory laudatory prefatory obligatory derogatory supererogatory interrogatory nugatory depreciatory denunciatory retaliatory conciliatory reconciliatory expiatory initiatory propitiatory dilatory oscillatory consolatory ambulatory adulatory congratulatory expostulatory amatory defamatory acclamatory exclamatory inflammatory confirmatory explanatory signatory hallucinatory minatory declaratory preparatory vibratory migratory respiratory expiratory oratory laboratory corroboratory accusatory excitatory hortatory salutatory lavatory conservatory factory olfactory satisfactory unsatisfactory manufactory refractory refectory rectory directory contradictory valedictory victory perfunctory introductory expletory prohibitory auditory monitory admonitory territory transitory depository repository desultory inventory promontory peremptory offertory repertory story history contributory circumlocutory interlocutory statutory savory unsavory ivory pry spry

rry

carry miscarry marry remarry intermarry parry tarry starry quarry berry huckleberry gooseberry blueberry blackberry mulberry cranberry raspberry strawberry dewberry bayberry ferry cherry sherry jerry merry terry equerry lorry sorry worry curry scurry furry hurry blurry flurry slurry

try

try podiatry idolatry barratry gadgetry rocketry basketry musketry toiletry symmetry geometry biometry trigonometry hygrometry poetry puppetry retry coquetry banditry punditry summitry paltry peltry deviltry poultry sultry pedantry infantry gantry chantry gallantry pantry pleasantry peasantry entry subentry reentry gentry carpentry sentry wintry country upcountry bigotry zealotry helotry harlotry pastry ancestry tapestry forestry vestry registry sophistry chemistry palmistry ministry dentistry artistry casuistry industry

ury

bury rebury mercury fury augury jury injury perjury penury floury treasury usury century luxury wry awry outlawry cowry dowry porphyry

sy easy uneasy greasy queasy idiosyncrasy fantasy ecstasy apostasy woodsy sudsy geodesy cheesy prophesy poesy heresy courtesy discourtesy cutesy daisy noisy hypocrisy clerisy pleurisy folksy palsy minstrelsy whimsy flimsy clumsy pansy tansy teensy weensy quinsy argosy nosy choosy posy rosy prosy leprosy catalepsy epilepsy tipsy biopsy necropsy dropsy autopsy gypsy controversy horsy pursy embassy gassy classy glassy massy brassy grassy sassy messy dressy missy prissy sissy bossy flossy glossy mossy fussy hussy pussy patsy bitsy ditsy antsy artsy curtsy gutsy busy lousy jealousy mousy newsy blowsy drowsy frowsy

aty treaty entreaty sweaty platy throaty nicety sleety safety fidgety gaiety dubiety society nimiety moiety piety impiety contrariety variety inebriety sobriety insobriety notoriety propriety impropriety satiety anxiety rackety rickety subtlety ninety snippety entirety surety velvety gayety crafty drafty hefty lefty fifty shifty nifty thrifty lofty toplofty softy eighty weighty flighty mighty almighty haughty naughty draughty doughty droughty

ity probity acerbity city perspicacity edacity audacity sagacity salacity tenacity pugnacity pertinacity capacity incapacity rapacity opacity veracity voracity loquacity vivacity periodicity publicity felicity infelicity catholicity multiplicity simplicity complicity duplicity tonicity electricity eccentricity authenticity elasticity domesticity causticity rusticity toxicity precocity velocity ferocity reciprocity atrocity scarcity paucity oddity heredity rabidity acidity placidity viscidity lucidity rigidity turgidity validity solidity stolidity timidity humidity rapidity vapidity intrepidity tepidity insipidity torpidity cupidity stupidity aridity acridity putridity fluidity liquidity avidity fecundity profundity commodity absurdity nudity crudity deity he homogeneity

lity technicality practicality impracticality locality rascality modality sodality ideality reality unreality legality illegality regality prodigality frugality lethality artificiality superficiality provinciality cordiality geniality congeniality materiality immateriality substantiality potentiality partiality impartiality bestiality triviality conviviality joviality formality abnormality banality venality finality originality criminality nationality rationality irrationality conventionality personality tonality principality liberality illiberality generality morality immorality neutrality plurality nasality universality causality fatality hospitality vitality mentality sentimentality instrumentality totality mortality immortality brutality duality individuality quality equality inequality sensuality actuality punctuality spirituality sexuality fidelity infidelity ability probability improbability applicability amicability practicability revocability malleability affability navigability sociability unsociability liability amiability variability availability controllability inflammability conformability inability attainability capability incapability palpability impalpability reparability invulnerability inexorability durability disability advisability respectability excitability inimitability irritability suitability unsuitability inevitability adaptability acceptability unacceptability stability instability refutability mutability immutability inscrutability equability conceivability immovability

debility irascibility miscibility credibility eligibility intelligibility incorrigibility indelibility fallibility infallibility gullibility feasibility divisibility sensibility insensibility extensibility responsibility reversibility accessibility impressibility compressibility admissibility remissibility permissibility possibility impossibility incompatibility perfectibility destructibility susceptibility digestibility flexibility inflexibility mobility immobility nobility volubility facility imbecility docility agility fragility nihility humility senility sterility puerility virility volatility versatility contractility gentility motility fertility hostility utility futility inutility tranquility civility incivility servility jollity nullity polity frivolity credulity incredulity sedulity garrulity

	amity calamity extremity dimity sublimity pusillanimity magnanimity unanimity equanimity proximity enmity comity infirmity deformity uniformity conformity
mity	

nonconformity enormity anonymity urbanity profanity humanity inhumanity inanity sanity insanity vanity obscenity lenity amenity serenity dignity indignity malignity benignity vicinity affinity infinity virginity salinity masculinity femininity trinity consanguinity divinity indemnity solemnity maternity paternity fraternity eternity taciturnity unity immunity community impunity disunity importunity opportunity pity uppity

	barbarity solidarity vulgarity charity familiarity peculiarity clarity hilarity similarity dissimilarity polarity particularity jocularity regularity irregularity angularity
rity	

singularity popularity parity oviparity imparity disparity rarity celebrity alacrity mediocrity sincerity insincerity legerity celerity temerity asperity prosperity posterity austerity dexterity verity severity integrity authority seniority inferiority superiority priority majority minority sonority sorority security insecurity obscurity purity impurity maturity immaturity futurity obesity falsity density immensity propensity intensity verbosity jocosity preciosity grandiosity curiosity animosity luminosity adiposity pomposity generosity porosity monstrosity sinuosity impetuosity varsity adversity diversity university perversity necessity sanctity quantity entity identity nonentity chastity acuity vacuity perspicuity assiduity ambiguity contiguity exiguity superfluity ingenuity continuity discontinuity annuity equity inequity ubiquity obliquity iniquity antiquity propinquity fruity congruity incongruity fatuity gratuity perpetuity fortuity

vity cavity concavity gravity depravity suavity longevity levity brevity acclivity declivity proclivity passivity impassivity nativity activity inactivity objectivity subjectivity conductivity productivity captivity perceptivity festivity laxity complexity perplexity convexity prolixity fealty realty specialty penalty commonalty severalty admiralty salty casualty loyalty disloyalty royalty cruelty novelty frailty guilty faulty faculty difficulty scanty shanty panty guaranty warranty plenty aplenty seventy twenty sovereignty dainty certainty uncertainty flinty pointy squinty jaunty bounty county runty maggoty booty snooty sooty empty nonempty arty hearty party nonparty warty liberty puberty property poverty dirty thirty flirty forty sporty sty yeasty hasty overhasty nasty dynasty pasty tasty modesty chesty majesty amnesty honesty dishonesty testy travesty zesty pigsty feisty misty sacristy twisty frosty thirsty bloodthirsty busty dusty fusty gusty lusty musty rusty crusty trusty batty catty fatty chatty natty patty ratty bratty tatty squatty jetty petty pretty ditty kitty gritty witty dotty knotty snotty potty spotty smutty nutty putty rutty beauty duty gouty deputy sixty

uy-zy buy overbuy guy obsequy obloquy soliloquy colloquy heavy navy gravy wavy bevy levy ivy chivy privy envy anchovy groovy nervy curvy scurvy savvy divvy chivvy dewy chewy sinewy screwy shadowy showy billowy willowy

snowy marrowy galaxy waxy apoplexy sexy pixy oxy boxy
orthodoxy foxy epoxy proxy sleazy hazy lazy crazy wheezy breezy
frenzy bronzy cozy dozy oozy boozy floozy woozy ditzy glitzy ritzy
chintzy klutzy gauzy blowzy frowzy jazzy snazzy dizzy fizzy frizzy
tizzy fuzzy muzzy

23. WORDS ENDING IN LETTER - Z

Z topaz adz jeez fez oyez biz whiz quiz ersatz kibitz ditz blitz fritz schmaltz waltz chintz blintz quartz hertz kibbutz futz klutz jazz razz fizz frizz buzz abuzz fuzz

www.ingramcontent.com/pod-product-compliance
Lightning Source LLC
Chambersburg PA
CBHW080249030426
42334CB00023BA/2758